M W
& R

ASK ME ANYTHING

Love, Sex, and Relationships in the '90s

Rhona Raskin

Macfarlane Walter & Ross
Toronto

Macfarlane Walter & Ross
37A Hazelton Avenue
Toronto, Canada M5R 2E3

Canadian Cataloguing in Publication Data

Raskin, Rhona
Ask me anything : love, sex, and relationships in
the '90s

Includes index.
ISBN 1-555199-003-2

1. Man-woman relationships.   2. Sex.   3. Love.
I. Title.

HQ801.R345   1996   306.7   C96-931811-1

The publisher gratefully acknowledges the support of
the Canada Council and the Ontario Arts Council

Book design and typesetting by James Ireland Design Inc.

Printed and bound in Canada

To my parents, Norma and Jack Raskin,
the first people I ever knew
who had a sense of humor about sex.

Contents

Introduction

I confess: this book is created out of guilt. For years on my radio show, whenever someone called in with a really unusual question, I would find myself ending the answer with something like, "Gee, that's a great one for the book." I meant it half in jest, but before long, people began asking where they could buy the book. They usually asked while they were on the air live, which at first left me stuttering and stumbling for a quick answer. Soon enough, I came up with one: I'm still working on the book, and as soon as it's ready, I'll let you know. Of course, this meant I actually had to write the damn thing, despite being far more familiar with the spoken word than with the written. Fortunately, I have a writer in the family (my brother, Avery Raskin, take a bow), and he grudgingly agreed to give me a hand, translating my radio ramblings into something more prose-like. You are holding in your hands the result.

My personal path to this book began as a case of mistaken identity. I was working as a family therapist when I got a frantic call from a Vancouver radio station — they had abruptly lost their open-line sex show host. I agreed to fill in on a temporary basis, and arrived at the station the following Sunday. A producer showed me the room in which I was to work, said something about the control board being roughly the same as one I'd used at another station, and headed for the door. I reminded her that I had never been on radio before and wouldn't know a control board from an emery board. That's when all of the blood left her face and pooled around her ankles, where it has remained until this very day.

For the next year, she showed me how a radio show operates, thereby ruining fifty-two consecutive Sundays that she could otherwise have spent at the beach. Eventually, a new radio station opened in town and asked me to expand my show to five nights a week from one, and from one hour per week to six. The next step was national syndication, which meant another change of venue, and upping the time-commitment ante once again — this time to fifteen hours a week.

My supporters over the years say my radio show and newspaper columns are funny and therefore entertaining. My detractors have complained that I don't take my callers' concerns seriously, because I'm always making wisecracks about their problems. My attitude is that giving out information in the style of a college lecture leaves people uninterested, bored, and hunting for the nearest exit. I find that I'm more open to learning new things if I'm relaxed and having a good time, and hopefully a good laugh. I've learned to understand that life is a journey, not a destination, and to appreciate the struggles along the way.

I was fortunate enough to grow up in a family with a casual, light-hearted, and occasionally twisted outlook on sexuality (you could find *Playboy* magazines scattered around my house, and no one who lived there had a second thought about it). This came in handy when I started physically developing at age ten, and suddenly had to deal with protruding body parts that could not be found on any of my friends. My abrupt and early entry on the fast track to an adult body left me asking why these things were happening to me, why these things were *only* happening to *me*, and how I could stop these things from happening to me. I eventually accepted my physical changes, especially since they soon stopped dead in their tracks. (My body parts are the same size now as they were then, right down to height, weight, and yes, bra size. Oh well.)

Despite rumors to the contrary, I was never an advice prodigy. I have managed to have just as many problems in my life as anyone who calls my show. For example: How to explain to my parents my unplanned one-week school vacation, earned by my "insolent behavior" during English class? Is it legal for him to send me a dozen red roses on my birthday and break up with me two hours later? Why is it that seven years of ballet lessons could never cure me of lurching into door jambs? Eventually I would discover the answers to these problems. ("See, it's an extra spring break." "Yes." And "Genetics . . . must be genetics.") I also noticed that I seemed to be attracting the problems of others, especially total strangers.

I suppose it was inevitable that I would end up in a field where I would get paid for what I was already doing, which perhaps explains the journey from youth worker to counselor to social worker to family therapist and registered clinical counselor. My private practice went public with the first one-hour radio talk show, later to grow to three hours a night, five days a week, from coast to coast. Add to that the syndicated newspaper column, and now this book.

Our relationships, our sexuality, our lives are much too complex to be tied up neatly in a single book, no matter who wrote it, so I haven't tried to accomplish the impossible. Instead, in the next few hundred pages, I have attempted to shed some light on the questions that have come up over and over again in my shows and columns, as well as the one-of-a-kind problems that got me saying, "Gee, that's a great one for the book."

1

Connecting

The beginning of any romantic relationship is wonderful, because everything is novel. You have no idea what her favorite color is, what he likes to do, what foods she adores. It's like setting foot in a brand-new world. Everything is fresh and bright and exciting. Not only that, but with someone new, you can *be* whoever you want, because this person has no history with you. If you choose to be witty and glib, there's no comedy cop hanging around going, "Aw, you're not that funny. What are you trying to do, impress him?" A new beginning is the ideal opportunity to bring out different parts of your personality.

Of course, the downside here is that you must be careful which options you pick at the outset of a new relationship. The person you're getting to know will expect things to always be as they were at the beginning. Imagine you start out with a Sunday routine of roses on the pillow beside her sleeping head, followed by a stint in the kitchen to prepare her a sumptuous Eggs Benedict. You've just set her up to count on wondrous weekend breakfasts for the rest of your time together.

A new relationship is wild and wonderful, but also has its problems. Because you have no experience with this person, you don't really know who he or she is. Knowing someone's ancestry and hometown and favorite vacation resort might tell you something, but in the beginning, everyone is on their best behavior. It's rare that people put their worst personality traits on display on the first or second or third date. It will be a while before you discover he wakes up in the morning with the worst case of jungle mouth this side of the Amazon, or that she hates family gatherings and will do anything to get out of attending yours.

New relationships also give rise to much confusion and countless dilemmas, and some of the most frequently asked questions I get from listeners and readers have to do with starting off on the right foot.

I recently had a first date with a woman I really like. I took her to this fancy French restaurant and it just seems like everything went wrong. Can you tell me some better places for first dates?

An intimate French restaurant may not be the worst place for a first date, but it's certainly in the top ten. It quickly becomes obvious if the two of you don't have a lot to talk about, as well as very uncomfortable. There's the incredible awkwardness of two people, seated across a starched white tablecloth, not talking. Meanwhile, the waiter hovers nearby, poised to interrupt at the precise moment you finally come up with something to say. Leave the candlelight and high-priced wine list for much later in the relationship, when you're already deep into the romance and want to be left alone.

For a first date, you're best off in busy, crowded places. The bustle will cover any stilted silences, and if there's shyness between you, it won't be as obvious. Go for one of the many restaurant chains that combine quick, simple eats with visual and auditory effects. If your conversation isn't stellar, you'll have a supply of new topics literally staring you in the face. And if all else fails, these eateries also offer a built-in first-date back-up system: friendly waiters ready to tell you their life story and ask about yours, thereby starting a conversation for you.

If dinner sounds like too much for your debut date, hit a coffee bar instead. It's casual, carries no expectations, and comes with a time limit. No one expects a coffee date to continue for hours on end — that makes it a good way to dip your toes in the pool of a new relationship and test the waters before diving in. There's also less potential for disappointment in the java date. A coffee connection that leads nowhere leaves you change from ten bucks, and no buyer's remorse.

There's a girl I want to ask out to a hockey game, but I don't know if she's much of a jock. If she's not, I'm afraid I'll blow my big chance. What should I do?

Go ahead and ask! It doesn't matter whether women are fans or not — it's an adventure to go to a game with a guy, especially if the seats are close enough to actually see what's happening. This also creates conversational possibilities: you explain the ins and outs of the game, she asks you a bunch of silly questions, your answers make you look brilliant. If things go well, you can always hit a café afterward for coffee and dessert.

Museums and exhibitions make great dates as well, even if you're not the artsy type. You wander around and peruse the information cards on the paintings or dinosaur bones — instant conversation starters. If you're really tongue-tied, you can stand in front of a piece, gaze intently, and drink in its deep nature. Or at least pretend to do this while you ponder what to say next.

When all else fails, there's always the old reliable first date: a movie. While you're waiting for the show to start, you can talk about the actors or the Oscars or why you like Fellini or Woody or Arnold. During the movie, of course, it's bad form to talk, so your shared silence is actually a good thing. Once the final credits roll, you can dissect the plot over coffee and dessert.

 I'm shy and just moved to a new city. How can I get lucky?

First of all, I think you're putting the eclair before the main course. Before worrying about where you're going to park your penis, perhaps you should try getting to know some people in your new hometown. This will lead to friendships and other kinds of relationships, including those where genitals are required.

One way to accomplish these goals is by volunteering to help people. Doing things for others is a great way to stop being the outsider. Think about it: the other volunteers obviously like interacting with strangers, or they wouldn't be doing just that, for no pay. If you're politically motivated, a campaign can be a great place to meet people. Politics leads to passionate debate, and sometimes passionate debate leads to passion, period (especially if you're on the same side).

Once you belong to a group, you meet people. The people in the group may not include your true-love-to-be, but one of their cousins, friends, siblings, or next-door neighbors might be. You'll end up at meetings and parties and outings to which you otherwise would not have been invited. Forming this new network for yourself takes only one simple act and requires only a bit of patience. After that, your "luck" should improve.

I've been dating a guy I really like for six months now. How do you know when you're really in love?

Humans seem to be the only creatures on planet Earth known to actually fall in love. Most species have sex and reproduce, but they don't seem to feel romantic attachment in the way we know it. When is it true love? I once heard it put this way: an indication of being in love is that when you're with that special someone, you really like who you are. In other words, your partner brings out the best feelings in you — you feel good about yourself.

According to Dr. Michael R. Liebowitz of the New York Psychiatric Institute, one of the biggest signs of falling in love is a feeling of euphoria, not unlike that created by certain drugs. You feel giddy or high. This is due to the release in the brain of a chemical called phenylethylamine, a chemical also found in chocolate. Of course, this means that sometimes when you think you're falling in love, you may just be craving a Hershey bar.

Other times, you may be getting your emotional signals crossed, as Dr. Lyn Alden found out in her famous experiment at the University of British Columbia. Alden had an attractive woman stop men who were crossing one of two different bridges, and ask them to participate in a survey. In the course of all this, she gave each man her phone number. The study showed that the men who had just crossed the rickety, swaying suspension bridge were much more likely to call this unknown woman for a date than the men who had chosen the low, safe bridge. Dr. Alden concluded that the reactions we get from being in perilous situations (racing heart, sweaty palms) are very close to how we feel when sexually excited or in love. This gives new meaning to the old expression "Look before you leap."

I don't have trouble meeting guys, I don't have trouble with dating, but things always seem to get bogged down over the whole sex thing. When do we do it, how do we do it, where do we do it, how do we protect ourselves when we do it? Sometimes it's enough to turn me off the whole subject. Why oh why is sex such a big deal in our society, anyway?

One of the reasons sex seems so all-powerful is that it's society's great equalizer. Rich or poor, young or old, no matter your ethnic group or geographic background, everyone can enjoy it. There is no training necessary, no exams to pass, and we are born with all of the equipment necessary for its enjoyment. With the right person at the right time, it is the most fun two people can have without laughing (as a stand-up comic once said), and you don't even have to be good at sex to love it.

On the genetic side, we are probably preprogrammed as a species to enjoy sex. As a mechanism for achieving closeness between people, of course, it's a biological imperative necessary for the survival of the human race, through reproduction. In the best of circumstances, sex is the ability to connect with another person on a deep, intimate level, and to do so while having an enormously wonderful time.

I get the feeling a girl in my psych class likes me, but I'm worried that my imagination may be working overtime here. How can you tell when someone is really interested in you?

You probably have no trouble telling whether you're well liked by teachers, cousins, and employers — use the same radar that gives you those answers to determine whether your classmate is interested at all. If you decide she *is* heading in your direction, you can check for further clues, by watching for the universal human characteristic known as "being a flirt."

Researchers at the Max Planck Institute in Munich spent years studying the flirting behavior of the human animal, and discovered common characteristics, regardless of the culture in which people were raised. The results say you can watch for: (1) A smile and a bashful look, followed by lowered eyes and a head turned away. (2) A gaze held longer than usual. (3) Repeated small touching movements. (4) A tendency to stand closer to you than a person normally would. (5) A mouth that's slightly open, and a habit of nodding in agreement no matter what you say. (6) A willingness to face you head on. (7) Use of the hands for emphasis. (8) Frequent checking of others' reactions to what you say. (9) Moistening of lips. (10) Choice of subjects of conversation on which you are likely to agree, rather than argue. If the girl in your psych class exhibits many of these "symptoms," she's very probably interested in you. Either that, or she's practicing to be a TV talk-show host.

When I meet a girl I like, I don't know how to find out if she's available. Can you suggest some way, without coming on like a sledgehammer and asking, "Are you sleeping with anyone?"

Try introducing the concept of the significant other in a casual way, such as "Does your boyfriend attend any of the same classes as you?" or "If you need a lift, I can drop you on the way, or are you expecting your boyfriend to pick you up?" If she is a boyfriend-free zone, she will probably let you know — unless she doesn't want additional attention from you. In that case, you'll get this kind of answer: "No, he's not, but I'm meeting someone later."

Q **At what age do you think it is okay to begin a sexual relationship?**

A There is no magic age at which it's okay to begin a sexual relationship, but I can tell you what is *not* a good age: thirteen or fourteen or fifteen, and not merely because your body is still growing. In your early teenage years, it's unlikely you've had enough life experience to distinguish things that are important from things that are not. You also probably can't decipher the subtle innuendoes in human relationships yet. We all need to learn a lot about human interaction, and once you become sexual, you tend to turn off the necessary receptors. That is one reason why teenagers sometimes make bad choices about their sexual partners.

In North America, most people become sexually active by the age of seventeen, but *most* does not mean *all*. There are a lot of men and women in their twenties and even thirties who are still virgins, and that works really well for them. Virginity is not a dirty word, and there are many advantages to it. For openers, you can sleep nights without worrying that you might be pregnant or carrying a sexually transmitted disease.

The best time to begin a sexual relationship is when you really care about the one you're with, when it's someone you know well, when you've already given the idea careful consideration, and when you've obtained protection to minimize the risky side.

Q **I'm eighteen and a high school senior, and my boyfriend is pressuring me to have sex. He says everyone our age is doing it. Are they really?**

A No, everyone your age is *not* doing it. In fact, not all married people over thirty are doing it, let alone single teenagers.

First of all, never let anyone pressure you into doing anything you don't want to do. Second, don't feel bad about not knowing every sexual statistic in the world by heart, because many people know a lot less than that. When the Kinsey Institute tested the sexual literacy of North Americans, they discovered most people have no clue. To give the example most relevant to you, when asked to pick the age at which the average person first has intercourse, most guessed between thirteen and fifteen years old. The actual average is two to four years higher.

So yes, there are lots of people your age having sex, but that doesn't mean you have to be one of them. If you're not comfortable with the idea for any reason, your boyfriend — if he truly cares for you — will respect your views. I can also tell you that in the last few years, I have spoken with many more twenty-two- and twenty-five- and thirty-five-year-old virgins than you could ever imagine existed. Until the time is right for you, it's the wrong time to start having sex.

Q **This is probably something you hear more from women than men, but here goes. I'm a twenty-seven-year-old virgin, and I'm terrified of where my life is going. I've had relationships with women, but when it comes to sex, I always break it off before things go too far. It's not a religious thing, I just thought I was saving myself for the "right woman," but now I'm starting to worry. If I finally do meet her, will she think I'm some kind of freak? Should I lower my expectations?**

A If you've waited twenty-seven years to sleep with the right person, I wouldn't leap on the bones of the next woman who passes by just because you're going to be twenty-eight. You'd be undoing all the groundwork you've put down to this point. After waiting this long, another couple of months — or years — makes little difference.

I don't know when, or even if, you'll ever meet the "right woman," but if you're second-guessing your desire to "save yourself" for her, you might examine your own background. We get a lot of messages about sex as we grow up — from families, friends, and communities. It's possible the messages you received didn't portray sex as particularly user-friendly. I don't think lowering your expectations is a great answer to your dilemma, but if abstinence is starting to bother you, go back and ask yourself some basic questions. What do you think sex is all about, and with whom do you think you should have it? Answer those, and you'll be a lot closer to deciding whether your belief structure needs changing.

I'm a single mother in my late twenties. Like many women who have had children, I have a little padding, but I'm not fat. My problem is that when I go to the bars with my girl-friend (who is slim and trim), the guys are all over her and totally ignore me. I don't have low self-esteem, I think I'm a good-looking woman. What's wrong with the men out there?

It sounds like you have a good attitude but are taking it to the wrong places. In one study, a researcher cruised the club scene and timed the conversations that occur there. The study concluded that the average bar chat lasts seven seconds. What can you possibly find out about someone in seven seconds? If your answer is "Nothing," go to the head of the class. I'd suggest you try a setting where you can have a real conversation. I predict you'll find more interesting men.

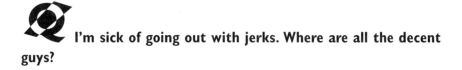 **I'm a newly single guy, and it's been so long since I've dated, I don't know where to start. I hate singles bars but I'm not sure where else one goes to meet new people.**

The best places are those where you'll meet the same people repeatedly over time. That way, you get to know them a little before you take the plunge and ask for a date. You may know a couple who met and fell in love while waiting for the bus, but they're the exception to the general relationship rule. Most people consider others strangers until they have some thread of connection. Either they've observed them for some time in a common surrounding (like a ceramics class, or a gardening club, or a bookstore), or they've been introduced by a mutual friend whose next-door neighbor had an uncle who . . . I'm sure you get the point.

So take a night-school course, volunteer for the cause of your choice, let your friends know you're in the market. If you're truly energetic, throw a party, invite your single friends, and ask them to invite other single friends. In the resulting mix of availables, the possibilities will be almost endless.

I'm sick of going out with jerks. Where are all the decent guys?

They're probably in the cycling club, not the sports bar. They probably look more like Mel Gibson's dentist than Mel Gibson. They were probably at the last party you attended, but you looked right past them, as you craned for a peek at the muscle boy in the corner. They're probably living next door — you know, that guy you won't consider dating because you think he's too awkward, or the guy at the gym whose abs would not be featured in an infomercial.

If you want to find a decent guy, erase from your mind the media image of the perfect man. We're so conditioned by soap operas and advertising and Hollywood, we imagine that the ideal partner looks like Brad Pitt or Cindy Crawford. In reality, decent guys are all around you. They come in all shapes and sizes. They may be the men you think of as "good friends" — the ones you turn to for advice about other men. They may be driving a car that does *not* have a 500-watt stereo CD. They may not have a washboard stomach and perfect buns. Decent guys are everywhere. You just have to change the way you look for them.

Why do women go for guys with a mean streak, rather than the "nice guys" they say they're trying to find? My friends say, "You're a nice guy." The women I date say, "You're a nice guy, let's be friends." Is it true nice guys finish last?

Actually, you are myth-taken. In fact, nice guys finish first, though it may take the woman who deserves you a while to pick you out from the crowd. Sometimes, though, when a woman says, "You're a nice guy, let's be friends," she really means, "You're a needy guy and you're smothering me — go away." Needy guys are in your face all the time — bringing you flowers, putting you on a pedestal, always there, always calling, always available. You get the impression they've got no life and want to borrow yours.

Unfortunately, needy guys — and needy women — often don't realize what they're doing. They think of themselves as "nice" because they *are* nice. They also smother you like a blanket. If you're a guy, it's important to have your own life. It's important to say to your woman, "No, I'm not available this Saturday, even though I'd love to do that with you," or,

"Sorry, I'm going out with my friends tonight, even though sex with you is great. We'll have to wait till tomorrow."

A final thought: don't confuse a woman's "bad boy" with her life choices. At some point in her life, nearly every woman has one man who is everything her parents warned her against. Part of it has to do with breaking away from your family — dating someone who in no way resembles your mother, father, sister, or brother. In the end, though, it's usually a passing phase. Most women go for quality, and if you're a quality guy, you can bet that one of those women will find you.

I always seem to take up with the wrong type of man — a problem drinker — no matter what I tell myself at the start. Why do I keep repeating the same mistake?

We're doomed to repeat our mistakes until we finally get the message. We tend to be attracted to people who are familiar. That's why we tend to date people who in some ways remind us of our father, mother, brother, or sister. Some people think all women seek men like their dads, and all men look for women like their moms. Some recent research suggests that we all settle down with a replica of our mother. This may be closer to the truth, since even in this age of single-parent families and two-career families, it's still usually Mom who has the most impact on our early upbringing. Anyway, in looking for the familiar, we gravitate toward people who react in ways we understand and expect. We lean toward those with whom we can act in our standard old patterns, even when those patterns aren't particularly pleasurable. If you take up with someone whose makeup is totally alien, you feel out of place — you have no script, you don't know how to react.

Learning from past mistakes means not being lulled into thinking a man is right for you when actually he's just familiar to you. Take a long hard look at what doesn't work for you in a relationship. To break out of your pattern, view your potential mate as a whole, before you commit to one or more of his parts.

I'm nineteen, and I've started dating a guy who's twenty-five. My problem is that I'm very religious (he's not), and I don't believe in premarital sex. My question is, how and when do I tell him I won't sleep with him?

Now! Tell him now! Or were you hoping you could wait a while longer — say, until he has all his clothes off?

That part was easy. The trickier answer comes when you start thinking about your other problem, the one you glossed over, which is probably going to be much more difficult to solve. It's a safe bet that the religious differences between you will be a major factor in determining how long-term this relationship is going to be. I'd suggest you sit down with your new guy and start talking about how easily you'll each be able to accept the other's point of view.

I like this woman at work, and I want to ask her out. I'm having a hard time asking because she is a goddess, and if she turns me down, I'll still have to work with her, and that will be even harder. Should I ask her out?

Most people meet others in one of two ways: through friends, or through work. If you eliminate the workplace, you're cutting your chances of finding Ms. Right by 50 percent. My position is that some people have gone way overboard in defining sexual harassment in the workplace, and that fellow workers are fair game for dating, with two conditions: you're not her boss, and she's not yours. That said, if you're unsure she'll say yes, the best way to ask her out is to try something less risky, like asking her to join you for coffee. Start slowly, see if she's interested in working up to a deeper relationship, and don't let the fact that she's a co-worker put you off.

The only thing about your question that perturbs me is your calling her a "goddess." Trust me: first thing in the morning, before her shower, she looks every bit as mortal as you or me. I suggest you take her off the pedestal before you ask for that date.

I'm eighteen years old and a virgin. It's not out of choice or morals — I'm just not turned on by the guys I date (or don't date). In fact, I don't seem to be interested in sex at all. Is there something wrong with me?

Since you're a virgin, it's impossible for you to say with certainty whether or not you like sexual intercourse — and no, I'm not suggesting you run out and try it so you can decide. What you're probably reacting to is romantic interest from the opposite sex, and at eighteen, a lot of people are simply not comfortable in a romantic relationship. So the answer to your question is no. Having no interest in sex does not mean there's something wrong with you. Give yourself some time and space. When the right person comes along, you'll be interested. There's no sex-life standard to which you must subscribe, and there's no need to explain your position to anyone. Either there's chemistry between you and another person, or there isn't. Until there is, remember that virginity is not a dirty word. I get a lot more calls from people who wish they'd waited longer than I do from people who wish they'd hopped into the sack sooner.

This seems stupid, but there's a girl in my class I want to ask out, and I just don't know what to say.

It isn't stupid — your problem definitely makes the list of most-asked questions. For people having a hard time approaching someone to whom they're attracted, the stumbling block is usually the discomfort of the frontal assault, and the possibility of a humiliating response. So why not try a sideways approach instead? This person is in your class. That gives you something in common. Ask her about the course, ask her opinion of the teacher, ask to borrow a book or some notes. That last one is an especially good approach, because it means you have to see her again to return what you borrowed.

People like to talk about things they know about, or things they're interested in. Ask her a question to which you know she knows the answer. Ask her to meet for coffee after class to elaborate on the points she made. She won't find this approach suspicious or threatening — unless, of course, the class you're sharing is sex education.

As you become familiar with each other, you'll get a better sense of whether she'd like to go out. If you realize she isn't interested, has a boyfriend, is gay, or whatever, you've made that discovery without getting the dreaded turndown. If she *is* interested, you've already got the beginnings of a relationship before you go out for the first time.

I've become close friends with a man who declares his undying love for me, but he says much the same thing to other women who are supposed to be "just friends" of his. What's going on here? Shouldn't the love declaration be a little more intimate and unique than that?

A A lot of people say "I love you" when they really mean "I like you tremendously" or "I positively adore you, but I don't want to have sex with you." Other people save I.L.Y. for their romantic partner and immediate family. Don't make assumptions about the way this man uses the love-y language until you've observed him in action a little longer. Meanwhile, you might let him know that, however he likes to use the word, you'd prefer something unique if he's going to profess his devotion to you.

Q **A certain woman and I have been friends for about ten years, and my problem is that I now realize I want to be more than just friends. Neither one of us is seeing anyone else at the moment, but I'm not sure how she'll react if I just blurt out my new feelings to her. I also don't want to risk the friendship I value so much. Should I take a chance and tell her, or just try to forget the whole thing?**

A You don't have to announce your undying love over the PA system — at least not until you're sure it *is* undying love. What you're really after here is the okay to take your relationship further down the road. You need to find out whether the light is green, red, or amber, without losing face and without making her feel she has rejected you (her friend!). There's always the hypothetical approach: "Hey," you say, "I just saw this article that said the happiest love relationships are the ones that started as friendships. Too bad we'll never know if that's true." If she answers, "Why not?" — consider the light green.

If that doesn't suit your style, ask her for help finding a lover: "Gee, we're such great friends, I wish I could find a woman just like you. You know, someone who looks like you, acts like you, cooks like you. Do you have a sister I don't know about?" If she says, "Nope, can't help you," you can probably forget the whole idea. If she says, "I was going to ask you if you had a brother," you just might be headed where you want to go.

Q I've known this guy for a couple of months. He's told me he likes me a lot, and I've told him the same. I thought that meant we were starting a relationship, but it seems for him that was the end of it. Why do men do this? He makes me so angry I could spit but, stupid me, I still like the guy. Please help me!

A When people — men in particular — verbalize strong feelings for the first time, they sometimes feel embarrassed about it later. It probably took courage for him to say how much he likes you in the first place. Now he may feel his words have bound him up in obligation. If that's the case, he's being unfair to himself, and you can probably help him out of the jam. Tell him you feel great about your mutual feelings, but let him know you have no bigger expectations, now that those emotions have been expressed. Remember that saying he "likes you a lot" does not mean he loves you and wants to park his toothbrush in your medicine cabinet. Don't attach more meaning to the words than actually exists. The other possibility is that he was telling you a deeper relationship was not in the cards, but that he still likes you a lot — as a friend. If so, that will probably become clear very soon.

Q Two different men I know have both expressed a romantic interest in me. As if that weren't complicated enough, we're all very good friends. And to make the situation even

worse, I think I've got a thing for them both. The imp inside me would like to jump both of them, but I know there would be a bad end to that scenario. What can I do?

A Keeping in mind that there are six billion people on the planet, is it really necessary for you to have a romantic relationship with either of them? That's the first question to ask yourself. In an ideal world, perhaps you could try them both out, pick one as a lover, and keep the other as a friend who wishes you the best. Unfortunately, this is not an ideal world, and whichever one you date, the odd man out will probably feel hurt and uncomfortable around you. Unless you are sure that one of these two men is the love of your life, and unless you're willing to jeopardize all the friendships involved, you might want to leave both of them alone for now.

Have patience. Time is on your side. A few months up the road, who knows what may happen? One of them may move to another continent. The two men may grow apart as friends. You may decide one is the man of your dreams, the other like a brother. All it would take is a small change in the dynamic to make your choice much less risky, and that change could come next month, or next week.

Q **I've always been the fat kid on the block and it has made me shy with women. I'm doing something about my weight, but I still need some way to build up my self-esteem before I have any kind of relationship with a woman. Please give me your womanly thoughts about this — I'm tired of being lonely.**

A Good for you for working on your weight, but remember that no one is meant to look like a toothpick, media images notwithstanding.

The problem with surplus poundage is that after a certain point, it's not just how you look, but how you feel that's important. If your extra weight is uncomfortable, it's probably unhealthy as well.

As for being shy, causes vary from one person to the next, and the appearance of your body is but one of many. I'd suggest you attack your two problems at once: get involved in an activity that involves both exercise and meeting other people, a hiking club for example. You'll probably find that once you accept yourself, people around you will, too. Finally, don't set too many goals at once. Think about getting comfortable with yourself first, meeting people second, meeting women third, falling in love fourth, and having sex fifth. If you try to mix all these things into one goal, you're giving yourself way too big a project.

I'm a thirty-year-old guy, I'm too short, and I'm not very good-looking. I've had few dates and few opportunities, and I'm wondering about plastic surgery. My friends think I'm crazy and should be thankful for my good health and nice personality. What do you think?

If you think of yourself as an unattractive package, it is unlikely people will contradict your expert opinion. If you think well of yourself, you'll project a positive image to which others will respond — including women. Whether you're a high-rise or a three-story walk-up, what matters is who's living inside.

Unlike the actors who have portrayed them on the screen, many of history's renowned lovers were men of neither statuesque height nor enviable looks. By all accounts, Casanova was downright homely. Don Juan? Forget it. Women like style and humor and personality. Before adjusting your outsides, try taking care of your insides. It's your self-esteem that needs a makeover, not the package that encloses it.

Q I'm falling in love with my girlfriend, and we're thinking of having sex for the first time. The problem is that it's <u>my</u> first time, but not <u>hers</u>. I always knew she wasn't a virgin, but she explained her past experience as a result of being taken advantage of by an old boyfriend. She has since admitted this was not the case, and now I'm feeling hurt and angry. How can I come to terms with this?

A It's only human to wish that the person with whom you're making love was constructed just yesterday. Unfortunately, all people come with a history. I'd guess that, out of consideration for your feelings, your girlfriend attempted to explain her previous sexual experience as something that wasn't much fun for her. When she told you her ex took advantage of her, she may simply have been telling you she was talked into something for which she really wasn't ready.

As for your reaction to her sexual experience, feelings often come without warning or invitation. If you're hurt or confused, it's understandable. However, it's probably not a place you want to dwell for too long, because it will interfere with the new history you're making with your girlfriend. Coming to terms with your emotions means accepting the fact that she has a past, just as you do. The important thing is that she's with you because that's where she wants to be *now*.

Q Why do people immediately look for a new relationship when they're on the rebound? And how do you know when a person is on the rebound?

A Some people fear being alone so much, they prefer almost anyone else's company to their own. They feel as if they are only half of a whole — incomplete if not in a relationship. Never mind *second*-best, this kind of desperation can lead to settling for whoever happens to be available. A better approach is to leave some time between one connection and the next. Get to know yourself as a single person again: rediscover the joys of eating the last piece of pizza, and sleeping diagonally across the bed.

As for recognizing the situation in others, here are a few handy tips. If he keeps calling you by an old girlfriend's name, you know he's not over her. It's also a safe bet she's on the rebound if it's been less than two days since she broke up with the last boyfriend, if he can't cook his own dinner, or if she can't start her car without a guy showing her where to put the key. In other words, anytime a person is that helpless, odds are they haven't been on their own for long. Examine whether the person you're interested in is looking for a relationship, or for the other half of a set of bookends, just because they feel incomplete alone on the shelf.

Interestingly, "rebounding" seems a bit more common among men than women. This may be because guys often take longer to get into the intimacy of a relationship, so they also end up taking longer to get out.

Q **I've been going out with this girl for two weeks now. My problem is, how do I kiss her, and when? I know she probably won't be the one making the move, so that leaves me nervous and confused.**

A The first-kiss dilemma stems from the idea that a kiss stands alone. It's like one minute you're talking about the political stability of nation-states in the former Yugoslavia, and then zip — your lips are pressed against hers, and she's going, "But wait, wait — I still had something else to say!"

A kiss should probably be something that occurs within a continuum of action. First you let the person see that you're moving in closer, and you pick up on your radar screen how she's doing with that. Move in fairly slowly, and if you need more clues as to the reception you're about to get, try this trick: put your hand on her face — either the side or around the jawline. If she's not into kissing you, she'll probably pull away — *before* you close your eyes, pucker up, and are left feeling foolish. On the other hand, if she moves in closer as your hand touches her face, she's probably ready for the kiss. An added bonus here is that a gentle hand feels good to the person whose face you're touching.

I always feel awkward trying to start conversations with women I don't know. Can you suggest some good icebreaker lines?

I can suggest some lines not to use, like: "Hey, diddle-diddle, mine's in the middle. Where's yours?" Or: "Guess what? There's a party in my pants, and you're invited!" Bad taste aside, even the best snappy openers require equally snappy retorts, and if the woman you're approaching doesn't have one ready, you're liable to get the big chill. Unless you're good at monologues, the conversation grinds to a quick halt. Try using your humor and imagination in a less combative way. I know a guy who starts every approach with: "You know, you look just like the girl who sat next to me in grade two. You aren't from Montreal, are you?" Predictable? Perhaps, but he swears it works like a charm.

Just about any sincere question will get things rolling. "Were you at the game tonight?" "What do you think of our history professor?" "Who do you think is going to win the election?" If all else fails, mundane as it sounds, talk about the weather. It's the one topic on which everyone has something to say.

Q I'm shy, and I'm interested in a certain someone as more than just friends, but I'm not sure how he'll react to my desire for a change in our status. How can I let him know how I feel without risking our friendship?

A Don't let your shyness muzzle you, but don't use the "hold your breath and then blurt it out" approach either. My suggestion to find out whether he's interested is this: next time you're together, say, "You know, you're such a great guy — intelligent, good-looking, sensitive, sexy, creative. If we weren't such good friends, I could almost go for you." Now the ball's in his court. He might say, "Yeah, we'd sure never want to risk our friendship," or he might respond with something like, "Hey, who says I can't be had?" If you keep it hypothetical, and treat the matter with light humor, you should be able to find out where things stand without risking everything.

Q I've known my girlfriend for six months, and each of us has previously had a very bad marriage. We love each other, and I've asked her to marry me or move in, but she always says "Maybe" or "We'll see." We're going on a tropical holiday together to a place where several men she once dated live. How can I tell her I don't want her to see these men alone? And why doesn't she want to get married before we go and make it the honeymoon we both never had?

A If you were going to your own family reunion instead, would you be so anxious to get married? Or would sometime next year, maybe, be soon enough? Ultimately, though, it really doesn't matter whether your desire to rush down the aisle comes from insecurities over half-naked ex-lovers all over the beach. You still can't get her to marry you before she's ready, and it sounds like she isn't. If you really are meant for each other, your relationship will continue. When the time is right for both of you, you'll know it. Relax, enjoy your holiday, and do not follow her around like a bumbling private detective while she visits her friends. If you can't trust her, you shouldn't even be thinking of marrying her.

I've been going out with a really nice guy for about six weeks. Three nights ago we slept together for the first time. It was a disaster. He was all embarrassed when he left my apartment, and I haven't heard from him since. I think it's one of those male ego things and he's all weirded out over it. What should I do?

The first time two people have sex is often a disaster. Many a man's performance is less than stellar, then he kicks himself, thinking there must be something wrong with him. After all, suddenly he was in the fantasy he'd dreamed about for six weeks, and once he got on stage, he blew his part. That's why it's called performance anxiety. It may indeed be one of those "male ego things," and he may not be calling because he thinks you're disappointed. Phone him up and tell him how much you've enjoyed your time together. Make it clear that the debut flop was a minor interruption in an otherwise wonderful relationship. If you take the lead, you'll give him the opportunity to stop stewing over the first time, so you can both get to enjoying the second.

I am a single, active, forty-six-year-old man. I was hoping I would "click" with a woman and she would ask me out for coffee, but it hasn't happened. And I hesitate to make the first move, because today's women seem to distrust men. What should I do?

Why are you waiting for her to ask you out? What's wrong with you asking her out instead? Yes, these aren't the '50s any more, but you're still going to have to make the first move at least some of the time. Don't worry about her distrust, either. No one you invite out for a cappuccino and a muffin is going to think you're a lech — unless, of course, you leer at her over the buns.

I'm eighteen, gay, and in the closet. Do you think I should come out now, or wait until I'm in my twenties?

When, how, even *if* you make your sexual orientation public — these are all matters of personal choice. I can tell you that many people in their teenage years spend a lot of energy trying to define their selves, and one of the big self-identifiers is "I am *not* gay." That means that if you come out now, don't be surprised to receive a lot of negative, unsupportive reactions from those around you. You may want to consider opening up only to people who really care about you — those who are unlikely to have that kind of reaction. The last thing you need in your life is hurt and rejection around your sexual orientation.

There are also people who make it all the way through adulthood and never come out of the closet, except with close friends and family.

There are others who say to the world, "This is who I am," and let the chips fall where they may. Neither way is right or wrong; it's only right or wrong for the individual who must choose. Remember one thing, though: once you make an open declaration of your homosexuality, it's very difficult to retract it. Before you make a general public disclosure, if that's your choice, make certain you're convinced it's the way to go. You might start with some private, specific declarations to your closest friends and family, and see how it feels from there.

I met this guy and I think he's really sweet, but all of his friends are telling me to stay away from him. They say he's really bad news, he'll break my heart. I guess I'm happy his friends are trying to protect me, but when I'm with him, he seems so great. What should I do?

The first question to ask yourself is why his friends are giving you advice. You're a stranger to them, and he's their buddy, so why are they running him down behind his back? If he's such a heartbreaker and such bad news, why are they his friends in the first place? My guess is that rather than trying to protect you, they may be trying to protect themselves. Perhaps they see you as a threat: if he has a girlfriend, he'll have less time to spend with them. Maybe they just aren't sure they want to include you in "the group." Maybe they're just jealous because it looks like he's getting involved in a great relationship — with you — and they don't have it as good. You might want to take one of the group aside, and see if you can't get the real story out of him. Whichever way it goes, I'd take a long look at the situation before taking his friends' advice to heart.

A woman I know, Lisa, says she can't date me because her best friend, Carol, previously expressed an interest in me. Carol is nice, but I don't think of her romantically. I think I could fall for Lisa, but it seems like I won't have a chance unless I date her friend first. What should I do?

First, remind Lisa that you have a vote here, too. This is not a deli where the first person in line gets the freshest Danish. In fact, it's actually poor taste to date your ex's best friend, so obliging Lisa's wishes would only create a bigger problem for you later on.

If they really are friends, Carol will be happy that her friend is getting involved with you. She must approve of you, since she wanted to date you in the first place. As for Lisa's being worried about hurting her friend, I'd say we sometimes go to unwarranted extremes while trying to protect others' feelings. I'm sure Carol will get over her disappointment, and the three of you will be good friends together. If not, she probably wasn't a great friend to start with.

Five years ago, the man I'm seeing got his former girl-friend pregnant. Because they were both in school, they decided to give the child up for adoption. Now he shies away from sex, because he says he couldn't go through that again. I'm on the pill and I've reassured him every way I know how that I won't get pregnant. I'm afraid this wall of his is going to kill any chance for our relationship to succeed. What can I do?

It sounds like your potential lover is a potential client for counseling. I have no doubt that giving up a child for adoption when he was very young and first involved in sex was hardly cause for celebration. But he's older now, and he should be able to absorb the concept that bad things are not going to happen every time he has sex. You're on the pill, you've reassured him, he can back things up himself by using a condom and spermicide. It seems to me that you've done all you can. If he's unwilling or unable to sleep with you, I don't see a strong chance for the relationship to survive over the long term. Until he gets the help he seems to need in resolving this old wound, I'd suggest you hold off on registering a china pattern.

My face goes red every time I talk to a guy. I panic when I mispronounce a word or have to carry on a simple conversation. My shyness keeps me from making friends, or even asking questions in class. Any suggestions?

It sounds like your self-esteem needs some work. If you start to see yourself as valuable, others will, too, and much of your problem will be gone. Some cities have shyness clinics to help you along the road to feeling good about yourself, and there are certainly counselors everywhere who can help as well.

If you want a tip for right now, try things out in a mirror. Most people have no idea how they appear when they're talking to another human being. If you rehearse some conversation starters in a mirror, you'll be less likely to be stumped in public. Also, if you're meeting someone new and don't know what to say, ask lots of questions: "Where are you from?" "Who's your favorite professor?" "What's your opinion of the ski conditions in New Zealand?" People love to talk about themselves and express their opinions. The trick is to find the "on" button that will get them started, and take you off the conversation hook. The truth is that a good listener is the best conversationalist. Nod your head a lot, and smile. You'll do fine.

Q **A woman I care about is very shy. Is there any way for me to tell if she's in love with me? I am also quite shy, so I could use some help for myself as well.**

A Rather than trying to find out if she's in love with you, why not start with whether she likes you and wants to spend time with you. Don't jump ahead of yourself, muck things up, and then blame it on your shyness. If she's shy, too, get her to talk about herself by asking questions. Ask her about her time in elementary school, the town where she grew up, the first boy she ever had a crush on. Get her to talk about her life and you'll get to know her in the process. She'll probably end up asking you much the same questions and get to know *you* at the same time. Before you know it, you won't even remember being shy, and you'll probably be a long way toward knowing each other's true feelings as well.

Q **When I look into the eyes of any woman who claims to love me, all I see is a pain in the butt who wants to manipulate me into marriage, make my life a living hell, and nail me for alimony. If I had to choose between a wife and a hole in the head, I'd like the hole to be the size of a quarter. I might consider a long-term ménage à trois with two bisexual women, but I want to know what financial responsibilities I would have toward them if the relationship fell apart.**

A Dream on. Judging by your letter, I'd say you already have a hole in your head. At present, let's say you're hardly the kind of bargain who would attract not one but *two* women at the same time. Frankly, you have an attitude problem in need of severe correction before you'll find yourself in a loving relationship. For now, try to remember that when you make only sour faces, you're likely to attract only lemons.

As for your financial obligations, should you actually manage to find two women to accommodate you, your lawyer can draw up a pre-ménage à trois agreement that will outline what is expected of you after it's over.

I am a thirty-five-year-old SWM and find it very frustrating trying to meet single women who are not married, divorcées, single moms, or tremendously materialistic. Where do you go to meet unpretentious, energetic, genuine, fit, slim, attractive, good-hearted, monogamous, romantic, fun-loving women in this age of AIDS, phonies, gold-diggers, vamps, and money-draining social scenes?

I'm glad to see you're not too picky — all you want is someone rich, brilliant, and gorgeous who will take care of your every need. I'm wondering what *you're* going to do here: just show up? Can you pass this test of dating perfection? Try asking yourself what's wrong with single mothers, or women who were once married. What problems do these women pose for you that they're off your list?

It's no wonder you're having such a hard time finding a date. Your list of conditions is so long, you'll need the Hubble Space Telescope to find anyone who fits. Once you've broadened your sights a bit, you can begin looking for your dream woman just about anywhere around you. If you want someone who isn't dominated by money, try volunteer groups — people who help others on their own time are much less likely to be selfish, phony gold-diggers. Also, if you join groups whose interests you share, you'll be more likely to find a woman with whom you want to share your time. Just remember, though, the woman who makes nearly all your dreams come true may once have been married, or may have a child, in which case you may want to reconsider your quest for perfection.

For the past few months I've had my eye on this cute guy I see in the food fair, and I've noticed him checking me out, too. I'd like to ask him out for coffee or lunch, but I'd hate to be embarrassed or rejected. Is it okay for a girl to ask?

Oh come on! You don't need me to tell you this! Of course it's okay, and if you're worried about rejection, there's a simple way to warm up to the question. A food fair is the ultimate place to share a table with a stranger — the way it's set up makes the practice almost mandatory. Just sashay up and ask if he minds you sitting down. If he's really uninterested, he'll make some excuse about seventeen business people coming to join him momentarily. If he's interested, he'll say "Sure." If you feel really brave, try it even if you're the only two people in the place. Go for it.

I have known this man for the last three years, and for the last month he has been my lover. We get along great, he gets along great with my children, this is the first man I have been seriously interested in since my divorce four years ago. Unfortunately, he doesn't love me. He says he isn't ready for a serious relationship, doesn't want to hurt me, and has an unpleasant side he doesn't want me to see. I know these things take time, and he may never be able to love me. What should I do?

A Falling in love can indeed take time. Ask anyone involved in a successful arranged marriage (there are many more than you might think). What you'll probably hear is that they weren't in love in the beginning, but fell in love once they got to know each other. In those cases, however, there is a commitment, if you will, to fall in love. The man you describe doesn't have that commitment, so it's unlikely time will solve your problem. He says he's not in love, doesn't want a relationship, but likes having sex with you. This makes him an honest man, but not an available one. I'd suggest you go back to being his friend and get out of his bed.

Q **At a friend's Christmas party this year, I got to know a girl from my school a lot better, and was planning to ask her out. The next day I found out she was about to date another guy for the first time. Should I still ask her out, or forget the whole thing?**

A Yes, ask her out. A rumor that she might be having a first date with another guy doesn't necessarily put you out of the running. What if she doesn't date him? What if the date with the other guy is a bust? This is the ideal situation in which to gamble — you have nothing to lose. Right now, you don't have a date with her, and the worst that can happen is that you *still* won't have a date with her. See? Nothing to lose.

Q **I'm twenty-five, male, single, and find myself in a situation that's new to me. I recently began dating one woman, and now I've met another I'd like to ask out. There's nothing serious going on yet with either. Is it okay to date both?**

A Yes, with two conditions. Each should know you're dating another, and you should not be having sex with both of them. Just because you've been on a couple of dates with Woman Number One does not mean you've entered into some kind of exclusivity arrangement with her. Once you start mixing sex and intimacy into the equation, however, things begin to get complicated in a big hurry. At that point, there are also moral and ethical issues to be considered.

If you need to, date a million women. People sometimes meet and marry in a whirlwind. Then, twenty years later, they start wondering if they've missed out on something, and maybe they should start having affairs. Get your experience in as much as you can *before* you get serious, and you won't need second thoughts decades later. Date your brains out.

Q I started dating this woman recently after a year or so of total uninvolvement with the opposite sex. I already know she's not the love of my life, but I feel like at least I'm having some kind of relationship. Is that wrong?

A What you've got going is either a BTN (Better Than Nothing) or a friendly but purely limited relationship. If it's the former, you may be shortchanging yourself, because you're tied up and unavailable for something more meaningful. You only have one body. It can only be in one place at a time. If it's in a BTN, it's not going to be accessible for anything or anyone else. Rather than convincing yourself this woman is "okay for now," ask yourself whether you'd still be with her if someone more interesting was available.

The second possibility here is that you aren't "settling" for someone who really isn't too bad, but rather are involved in a fun, friendly relationship that just isn't "true love." If so, don't worry about it. Not every relationship in your life is going to be as deep as the Pacific Ocean. However, you'll be a more sophisticated person if the course of your life contains lots of dating and social experiences.

As long as there's no misunderstanding on either side about the scope of your limited relationship, there's nothing stopping you from enjoying each other's company. This kind of connection only gets into trouble when one party is busily falling in love and planning the marriage ceremony, while the other is looking at the clock and thinking it's time to find the nearest exit.

Unlike most of my circle of friends, I've never had a one-night stand. I know it's not a very safe idea these days, but couldn't I just have a couple, for the sake of experience?

No one appointed me arbiter of one-night stands. I'm not the one to decide — you are. You can latex yourself to minimize the chance of problems like pregnancy and sexually transmitted diseases, but nothing is 100-percent effective. That means that no matter how many precautions you take, you run some risk, and that risk is multiplied by having a stranger as a sexual partner.

If you really must have a one-nighter, I suggest you fool around in ways that are major turn-ons but fall short of intercourse. The safer alternative, of course, is to confine your sex life to someone you know well, but close your eyes and pretend it's a stranger — he'll never know the difference. As Quentin Crisp once said, "For flavor, instant sex will never supersede the stuff you have to peel and cook."

Q I've always had a hard time meeting women, and I'm thinking about looking into telepersonal ads. What do you think of them?

A Personally, I think telepersonals are impersonal. I think they can be a waste of time and money, despite the long list of people who I'm sure would tell me they met the love of their life using them. The bottom line is that some people meet their love match in a bathroom. That doesn't mean your best bet is to hang out at the soap dish hoping your soul mate will happen by.

Calling a stranger you've only read about in an ad may work for some of the people, some of the time. Unfortunately, it can also be a very expensive way to meet new friends. These are also the places where weird kinds of people can be lurking, just waiting for the unsuspecting to come along. You can't tell from the words whether a person is just shy and lonely, or has a criminal record as long as your left leg. You also can't tell if they're telling the truth. If you're going to use these services, be very careful. Don't give your new date your address or your phone number, arrange your first meeting in a public place, and be skeptical.

If you really want a decent chance of finding someone with whom you could fall in love, make up a list of all the different places and ways you can meet new people. Then try five or ten or fifty of them, *before* embarking on a course of commercially arranged blind dates. You'll meet more varied and interesting people in a grocery store, a night-school course, your cousin Louie's wedding, or a hiking club. Also, in any of those places, you can get references from someone on that new stranger you find fascinating.

Remember, anything can happen anywhere. There's an old theory of philosophy which says that if you put a bunch of monkeys in a room with a typewriter for a long enough time, sooner or later they'll re-create

Hamlet. That doesn't mean if you're interested in Shakespeare, you should buy a chimpanzee. The critter is far more likely to go ape on you than to create immortal literature.

Q **I'm in a relationship that is heading for Splitsville, not because of some incompatibility or infidelity, but rather because he is moving to a new city. He wants me to go with him, but all of my friends are here, and while I really do like him, it's only been two months. How can I decide?**

A It's rarely a good idea to pull up your roots and charge off into the distance with a man you've only known for two months, so hang on to your library card for now. If this is a strong relationship, being apart for the next few months will probably enhance it, rather than detract from it. There's a lot to be said for long-distance romances, like the rush of seeing each other when you do get together for visits. In eight weeks, you've only scratched the surface of this person, and you have no idea what he'll be like in the long term. Your main business now is to give yourself the time to discover whether he's the man worth giving up your hometown connections for. Don't be hasty, or you may have two long-distance moves in your near future: one away, and the other right back again.

Q **I'm having a first date with a girl I was friends with a long time ago. I'd really like to impress her but don't want to look like I'm trying too hard. She's coming over to my place — any suggestions? Did I mention I'm not a very good cook?**

A Try to make the date on a weekday — that way, you'll have less pressure than on an "official" Friday or Saturday night date.

Now for the preparation. Start with the props. Big soft pillows on the floor work well for comfort, and a show-and-tell item on the coffee table can be a great conversation starter: try a photo album of a great trip or a favorite video.

As for the dinner itself, don't worry about trying to become a grand chef overnight. The fact that you cooked at all will be impressive enough, as long as you stay away from macaroni and cheese. You can pick up some deli chicken, cook some baked potatoes, and use a prepackaged salad mix. Let her think you're healthy — get the Italian mix or the Oriental. Either will look great, especially if you add some stuff with color, like red peppers, for example. As for the salad dressing, just mix up some honey and Japanese rice vinegar. When it's on to dessert, partially thaw some raspberries and toss them over low-fat ice cream for a great combination.

Now that you're ready for her big arrival, dim the overheads and fire up some candles — the soft glow will make the humblest abode look inviting. Finally, remember to relax. There's no such thing as a perfect date, first or otherwise, and no one will rate your performance on the six-o'clock news. Enjoy!

Q I really like this guy at school, but the problem is he doesn't notice me. I'm not attractive, so what can I do to get his attention?

A "This Guy" sure seems to get around, because you'd be amazed how many letters I get from women who like him. Okay, let's look at This Guy: he's made up of the same molecular structure as you, and is therefore intrinsically no better or worse than you either.

If you believe you are unattractive, then you will be unattractive, but the opposite is true as well. Forget the magazine covers and movie screens: who you are and how you feel about yourself play much more defining roles in your attractiveness than your physical attributes. Change your hair or makeup or clothes if you like, but only as a shortcut to convincing yourself that you are indeed attractive. Once you believe it, others will, too. Don't forget the power of style. Find a look that is yours and wrap your package with it, instead of trying to squeeze your package into someone else's mold.

Once your self-image is in order, all you have to do to make This Guy notice you is walk up and say hello. You'll know in short order if he's a nice guy who is worth your time. A friendly gesture is all it takes to start things off, then you'll find out where it goes from there.

Here's a question I think every guy wants answered. What exactly do women think about when they see a good-looking guy go by? Is the first thing on their minds a sexual fantasy (like most guys when a woman walks by), or is it really more cerebral?

Not to give away any gender secrets here, but when a good-looking guy passes by, a sexual fantasy often doesn't even make the cut on a woman's mental top-ten list. Dreaming about how he'd be in bed probably falls around position seventeen, far below such things as "I wonder if he has a job," "I wonder if he treated his last girlfriend well," and "I wonder if he can afford to take me on a date that doesn't include a Pirate Pack."

Q **I've recently completed four months of treatment after escaping an abusive relationship. Now I think I'm met a pretty special guy, but I'm wondering if it's too soon to get involved again. What do you think?**

A If you've completed four months of treatment, you've probably received some kind of guidance about relationships that you can incorporate into your life. Often it's a good idea to leave some breathing space to be your own person when you're going through these kinds of changes — before you have to deal with the needs and wants and baggage of another human being. As long as you've given yourself enough time to understand what happened to you, what you want to happen differently in the future, and what it is you're looking for, then four months can be enough lag time to start a new relationship. On the other hand, if you feel undefined, unsure, and shaky, or you feel you're still reacting to and dealing with the business of your last relationship, then you might want to give yourself a bit more time and space to sort out those issues. In that case, you could still have a connection with this special person — just keep it more on the level of a friendship for now.

There is no timing device that can tell you when you're ready to be with another person, other than asking yourself questions about where you've been, and where you're heading.

Q **My best buddy just broke up with his girlfriend. I've always liked her. Their split was amiable and he's not really the jealous type, but I feel like I'd be tacky to call her up right away and ask her out. Is there some logical time period I should wait?**

A Unfortunately, there's really no rule of etiquette to determine when one can rush in to fill the void caused by someone else's having vacated a relationship. Emotions, friendships, and other ties are involved here, and they all complicate the equation. I'd suggest you ask your good friend how he feels about other guys dating his ex-girlfriend, and whether that would be difficult for him. Then ask how he'd feel if it was someone he *knew* who was dating his ex-girlfriend.

I'd hope that the connection with your best friend would be more important to you than the fact that you are attracted to his ex. And you should also consider that you're not in a unique situation. Being attracted to your best friend's girlfriend or boyfriend or ex is completely understandable when you look at the upside: you've already gotten to know and like and be liked by this person, in a relaxed situation, with no other strings attached. This is why, many times, the best relationships start out as friendships, which then develop into romance.

Once you've resolved the issues of your friend's feelings, the only caution you should take is to ask yourself how much of the attraction you feel for his ex is due to convenience. The once unattainable may suddenly be attainable. Would you have wanted to date her if you didn't already know her so well? If the answer is yes, you may be on the right track.

Q The guy I'm seeing seems to be the perfect man. He's kind and considerate and makes me laugh, and I'm just deliriously happy when I'm with him. The only thing that keeps me from thinking I've found Mr. Right is his past. I know that before me, he chased every woman in sight, and caught most of them. I guess I'm worried he'll revert from being this wonderful guy I know to the king of the one-night stand. Am I being unfair?

No, you're not. This is why humans have long-term memory — you're just using yours. The question you're asking is, can people change? The answer is yes. It's possible that Mr. Almost Perfect had enough variety in his life to realize that relationships are not found but made, and he's now trying to make one with you. Everybody has things in their past of which they're not particularly proud. If you feel he's a kind and considerate man with a wonderful sense of humor, you shouldn't toss his phone number out the window just because of his track record.

Since you have this information about his past, perhaps you could bring up the subject, see how he reacts, ask if he sees things differently now. If you feel more comfortable after that chat, you can more confidently let the past be the past, and get on with the present and the future.

I haven't had sex since I got divorced. (In fact, it was quite a while before that!) I'm not only worried about the chance of finding someone new, but even if I find someone new to have sex with, I'm afraid I'll be awful in bed.

Having sex is like riding a bike — you never forget how, you just have to be careful of the bar between your legs. I can't help you find a new bike, but rest assured, once you get in the saddle, it'll all come back to you.

I'm twenty-one and still a virgin. Although this is my choice and I'm not about to change my mind based on embarrassment, I feel really awkward when people find out.

A Why do people find out? You don't owe anyone an account of your sexual history or lack thereof, unless you are sexually involved with them. Obviously, you are not. There is a certain tyranny in questions. Just because someone asks, it doesn't mean you have to answer. It seems clear this is something you don't want to share, except perhaps with those people closest to you. In that case, I'd suggest you deflect the question, not because you should feel apologetic or ashamed about your virginity, but because it's nobody's business. You might respond: "Why are you asking me that question? How much money do you have in the bank?" Your sex life is just as personal as your financial situation, and you have just as much right to keep it private.

Q It's no secret to us guys that a woman's physical appearance is important. My question is, do women feel the same way about a man's body?

A First, a little science. Curiously enough, the research shows that what a man typically likes in a woman's body is not size or shapes of breasts or bums in isolation. Instead, men are attracted by a certain ratio of hips to waist to bust size. To put it simply, men like curvy figures, regardless of the size of the curves. Women, on the other hand, are willing to let the ratio slip farther from the ideal when it comes to their ideal man. For example, they tend to be a little more forgiving when it comes to thickening around the male waist. Women are a bit kinder in their ultimate fantasies about a man, and will settle for more of the reality of mankind, as opposed to the illusions on the big screen or in the pages of the magazines.

When it comes to judging our own bodies, and their perceived flaws, men are much more forgiving than women. To a guy, five extra pounds on the scale is just so much more muscle, and cause for acceptance, if not celebration. To a woman, five extra pounds is a disaster that ruins her whole day, and she certainly couldn't have sex with it holding her down. In other words, women flog themselves about their extra weight, while men parade around with their chests stuck out, thinking it just makes them that much more attractive. Of the two approaches, I think men are much more healthy in their personal outlook.

I can't stand it when other guys talk about women like they're sexual objects. I think it's a privilege for a man to be able to touch a woman. Why are some guys such idiots?

I'd like to meet your parents. Guys who genuinely respect women probably had some pretty good messages being delivered at home while they were growing up. Guys who don't, probably didn't.

Is there any scientific method to determine a person's true sexual orientation? I have felt drawn to both men and women on different occasions, and I've dreamed about gay (as well as straight) sex, but I don't really think I'm bi.

Many people think sexual orientation comes in three distinct flavors: heterosexual, homosexual, and bisexual. However, the Kinsey Institute's research points to individual sexual orientation actually existing along a broad spectrum. At one end are those who are only attracted to, and only have sex with, members of the opposite sex. At the other are those drawn only to people of the same sex. And right in the middle are those who under certain circumstances can be aroused by either. The Kinsey folks have devised a seven-point scale, and found that most gays and straights are actually 2s and 6s, not 1s and 7s.

Your own sexual orientation might best be defined as a combination of whom you have sex with, whom you fantasize about having sex with, and to whom you're attracted. Homosexuals sometimes have heterosexual fantasies, and vice versa, so your dreams may not really shed much light on the question.

Most experts these days believe your sexual orientation is set long before you have any major use for your genitals, and there is no known therapy capable of changing that orientation. Whether the orientation stems from genetics, environment, biochemistry, or whatever else is academic. The point here is that we're better off accepting who we are, rather than spending a lot of time and money trying to alter something that can't be changed.

I'm a woman in my forties, divorced for five years. I dated men my own age for a while, but I find I prefer younger men in my bed (mid-twenties). My friends are giving me a lot of flak over my "cradle robbing," but haven't men dated younger women for centuries?

Men have indeed dated younger women for centuries, and the idea of women dating younger men is finally gaining acceptance as well. Some of the changes are sociopolitical. Women used to be relatively powerless, so they looked for men with position and power, which tended to mean men who'd been around longer. Older men didn't need women to work or help out in the money department, so they tended to look for wives who were decorative — in other words, younger.

Today, women have more economic and societal power, so they're looking for someone whose company they enjoy — and that doesn't necessarily translate into someone older, wiser, and teacher-like. Let's face it: anyone given the choice of being twenty or eighty will pick twenty, so if you have the opportunity to hang out with some younger energy, there's something to be said for it. As long as both people are happy in a relationship, their relative ages are irrelevant. And it's nobody else's business.

I'm only five feet tall and very petite. My new boyfriend is well over six feet, and built like a football player. Things are going well, but I'm afraid that when we do try to make love he'll be too big for me. Do I have cause for concern?

Probably not. The stature of a man or woman generally has no correlation to the size of his or her sexual equipment. A very large man can have an average-sized penis, and a very small woman can have an average-sized vagina. Many people have been involved in short/tall relationships, of course, and one of the most frequent comments seems to be, "Lying down, all people are equal." You might actually find that the relative differences in your body sizes provide extra variety, and if one position seems awkward, there are many others you can try. I'm sure you'll find ways that work for both of you.

2

Staying Power

After you learn her favorite milkshake flavor, or the unusual way he likes to have his dress shirts pressed and folded, you're entering the next phase of your relationship. Things aren't so new any more, you've heard all the jokes he likes to tell at parties, and seen all the origami tricks she can do with table napkins. Some of your friends may still be enamored of your loved one's idiosyncrasies, but you find yourself yawning as the next joke, trick, or story begins. If the beginning of a relationship is the bold leap into exotic adventure, the middle is remembering to pack a spare roll of toilet paper and a list of common Spanish phrases. Things start to grate a bit in the middle of a relationship, like the way he leaves his socks all over the floor, or the way she fights like cats and dogs with her family — battles you may believe are partly her fault, though if you're smart, you don't tell her that.

The middle of your relationship is a survival test. The person you idealized and set up on a pedestal when you first met has come down to earth, flaws intact, and all the traits you once thought were so cute are now the bad habits you throw at your partner when an argument begins.

The middle of a relationship is where the road gets rockiest, but that doesn't mean the trip is a disaster. There's no greater feeling than accomplishment — knowing you set out to do something difficult, saw it through, and won out in the end.

My girlfriend is into all kinds of sports and has a lot of friends. I'm glad she's not a couch potato, but between tournaments and nights out with the girls, we don't get much time together. We've talked about marriage, but I don't want a wife I have to make an appointment to see. Am I wrong?

It's not a matter of right or wrong — it's a matter of what works. If you were a guy who likes to have lots of free time and your own set of friends to visit, the situation would be wonderful. On the other hand, if you're dependent on her to be the vital link in your social schedule, then you're in for disappointment.

There are a couple of remedies for this problem. First, you can get involved in some sports together. This will provide her with the athletic buzz she seems to need, and you with her company. Second, you can look for activities that interest you as much as sports interest her. Then you won't be sitting home in the evening, looking at your watch. You'll both have your extracurricular fun, and enjoy the time you do spend together.

This is not something that's really discussed by many couples, but spending too much time together is sometimes not conducive to a wonderful relationship. People who live in each other's pockets tend to get on each other's nerves. They have little to contribute to the relationship by way of new energy and new material. I believe it's important to have interests outside the relationship, and obviously she does. If you feel she's putting too much time into those outside interests, talk to her about it. Perhaps she'll be willing to give up this or that evening for the sake of your happiness, as long as you aren't expecting her to change her entire life in the process.

My boyfriend and I are going to be starting a long-distance relationship soon (he's being transferred by his company). How can I keep our flame lit over distance and time?

For starters, you have to keep the communication lines open. That means bigger phone bills, and maybe a trip back in time to letter writing. You can leap head first into the Internet world of e-mail, if you haven't already. Or you can ease into the techno-age with that halfway measure, the fax machine. The advantages of faxing your long-distance love are twofold. For one, he'll get to see your handwriting, the next best thing to hearing your voice. Second, you won't have the computer keys and screen getting between you and your dear departed. The advantages of e-mail over the Net are also twofold. The delivery time is even shorter than a fax, and there are no long-distance bills. You can also get into a private Internet Relay Chat channel, and message back and forth in real time, or get software that will enable you to use the Internet as a free long-distance phone service (this isn't a computer manual, and you should get the point by now).

Once you have the communication conundrum solved, the rest of your problem will more or less take care of itself. Assuming you've kept each other at a slow simmer while separated, once you get together things will really start boiling. Some people find long-distance relationships peter out quickly. Others find they work great because when you *do* have live visits, you tend to not waste time on petty bickering or routine chores, and really enjoy each other's company.

The bottom line: if you want your relationship to go the distance, you'll have to make a real effort to keep in touch. Communicate. And be sure there's a set ending to your time apart. If not, there may literally be no end to your separation.

My girlfriend and I have been together two years now, and we have only one serious problem. I have a lot of good-looking friends and she's always got her hands on them (knees, shoulders, backs). My buddies say I should just relax, but it bothers me. Am I just being unreasonably jealous, or should I tell her it's bothering me?

Doing the kind of touching you're talking about is called being kinesthetic, and different people react to it in different ways. Some are more comfortable with more body contact — moving closer, talking closer, touching an elbow or arm while making a point. Others are more reserved. Obviously, your girlfriend is one of those touchy-feely, kinesthetic types, and perhaps you're not.

Are you being unreasonably jealous? I don't know, but jealousy always seems to be a wasted emotion in any case. Should you tell her? Perhaps, if you're ready for the very real possibility that she may look at you with saucer-wide eyes and say she doesn't know what you're talking about. You say you have a lot of good-looking friends. Would you feel differently if your friends were ugly? You say she's always touching their knees, shoulders, backs. Does that mean you feel her touching is some preamble or invitation to more intimate touching later?

Remember that many people are comfortable with a friendly kind of body contact that has no sexual implication whatsoever. If you're not one of them, I'm not suggesting you take it up. I'm also not suggesting you ask her to keep her hands in her pockets when your friends are around. That would probably create a rift between you. I guess what I am suggesting is that you learn to love your girlfriend's way, and if that's not possible, then at least learn to live with it.

What's the best way to make sure your man never cheats — and I mean never!

You could try nailing one of his feet to the ground, or hiring a full-time detective, but there's really no foolproof way to make sure a guy never cheats. So where does that leave you? If you don't play the lottery, you can't win the prize. In other words, if you think there's a chance this relationship will grow into the love of your life, you'll probably have to trust him and see how it works out. At best, your dreams will come true. At worst, he will cheat, you'll kick him out, and — once you recover — you'll roll the dice on the next guy. It's entirely possible, I should add, that undue suspicion has killed more relationships than cheating.

My boyfriend has bad breath and it's driving me nuts. What should I do?

Your first option is to simply tell him his beastly bouquet must be curbed, or your closeness will be instead. Your second option is to send him to a bad breath clinic. Believe it or not, some universities already have them. To use the mouthwash term, halitosis can be caused by anything from eating too much garlic to dental or gum problems. Sometimes the cure is as simple as gently brushing your tongue and palate while you attend to your teeth. Remember to do it delicately, though — taste buds are sensitive little organs.

My wife isn't as interested in sex as she used to be, but my drive is still thundering along. Short of my making do with less, is there any way to equalize our desire levels again?

Relationships change as people get to know each other, but there are things you can do to keep the fire going. The last thing you want to do is to become predictable and have everything be exactly the same every time you have sex. What often happens in long-term relationships is that people stop trying. They just think, "Here are my genitals, there are hers, let's just put them together and do the old bangy-bangy thing until someone has an orgasm." You probably require more variety, and more setup time. Perhaps when you first met, all you had to do was look at each other across the room and passions would be inflamed. Now it seems to take a little more than that. Your life together can still be passionate, but I think you're going to have to put some work into it. Try treating your wife as if you just met her. Make a point of bringing back the romance in your relationship, and your sex life will probably take care of itself.

I love my girlfriend, but she really keeps me on the phone too long when she calls. How can I get her to hang up faster without hurting her feelings?

A If you're really sure you can't use the straight-out honest approach ("I love you, hon, but I can't stay on the phone all day"), then I guess you're going to have to go for the theatrical. For one, you can pretend you have call-waiting ("Someone's on the other line, I'll call you back"). Or you can crumple some paper next to the receiver ("Bad connection, love, but we'll talk later!"). If those don't work, try talking endlessly about the weather, or pick a conversation topic you know she hates ("I've just got to tell you about this fabulous match I saw on World-Wide Wrestling!"). Finally, there's always the old standby — "Gotta go, sweetheart — someone's at the door."

Q **My boyfriend and I are planning to move in together, but we have what seems to be an insurmountable problem. I love cats and think dogs are the lowest form of life. He loves dogs and thinks all cats should be drowned. I own a Siamese, and he's got a schnauzer, and if the two of them are in the same room for thirty seconds, it's World War III, animal style. I love my guy and he loves me. How can we resolve our pet peeves?**

A The most obvious solution is to get rid of either the Siamese or the schnauzer, and replace it with sea monkeys, which are compatible with either. Since most pet owners feel as protective of their animals as parents do over their children, this is also the most unlikely solution. Your next option is to acclimatize the dog and the cat. Believe it or not, canines and felines have been known to live together in harmony. If yours don't get along, you could try bringing them together slowly, for gradually longer time periods, with gradually shorter intervals in between. If building a relationship between your pets is important enough, you may *both* have to move from your homes, so that you can start fresh in a place about which neither pet feels particularly territorial.

Q **My girlfriend likes to have the lights on when we make love, and I like it dark. Can you help us resolve our problem?**

A Haven't you heard of a dimmer switch? Or candlelight? By the way, it's often the other way around — a lot of men I hear from like to see what's going on, while many women wish they had lingerie that went from their ankles to their eyebrows.

Q **My girlfriend is lousy in bed. I don't have the guts to say anything to her, like "Hey, this sucks" or "Hey, look alive," and I know it's not inexperience because she had plenty of sex before me. Oh my God, maybe she doesn't find me attractive!? Help me — she just lies there.**

A Don't get your equipment tied in a knot. Women don't generally sleep with men they find unattractive. If she's like most women, and she didn't like you, she wouldn't have *bad* sex with you, she'd have *no* sex with you. If she is not inventive enough for you, and you have some ideas, share them with her. Exploring is part of being sexual partners. Either tell her, flat out, what kinds of things you think might be fun, or just say, "Hey, why don't I get in the driver's seat tonight and show you what I like?"

If she's just lying around like a piece of bread, she may be having sex more often than she wants. It's also possible that she's not being honest with you about what exactly tickles her fancy, and what doesn't. Maybe you're not doing enough for her, but she's not comfortable letting you know that. It's very ironic that people who are willing to have sex with each other are often unwilling to talk about the sex they're having. At this point, you can either continue having dead-in-the-bed sex, or summon your courage, open up the issue in conversation, and see if you can't make your sex life more recreationally appealing.

I have a wonderful relationship with a wonderful man who has one major fault — he smokes. When we met, so did I, so it was no problem, but now I've been off the weed for a year and he's still puffing like a diesel locomotive. I love him dearly and I thought it wouldn't matter, but the more time goes by, the more it bothers me. His clothes stink, our apartment stinks, his breath stinks, and it's hard to even kiss him these days. What can I do?

You certainly can't make him stop smoking. Listing all the perils of smoking will in no way cause him to throw his butts to the ground and stomp on them. Anyone who is still smoking has heard all the risks, and a mere recitation of what might happen to his body is not going to be enough to make him quit.

Studies show that most people who do succeed in quitting practice a lot before getting it right. They may not quit for good the first or second time, but they may succeed on the third or fourth try. What you can do is encourage him to cut down, while he's on his way to quitting altogether. There are a number of products on the market that may help, and his doctor can discuss the merits of nicotine gums and patches with him.

The bottom line, however, is that all changes a human being makes to his or her life are made only when the individual person is ready for them.

They are rarely if ever made when their partner, mother, or next-door neighbor thinks they should be. You knew he was a smoker when you met him, and I guess from his point of view, nothing's really changed. Unfortunately, for you, that's the problem. Don't give up hope, however, that one day (soon?) he might decide to butt out.

The smoking habit is probably the focus of the most drastic turn-around trend in history, at least in North America. Whereas many movie heroes and heroines of the '30s, '40s, and '50s were portrayed as coolest only when a cigarette was dangling from their lips, our heroes today tend to shun the taste of tobacco. What was once considered cool and trendy is now branded unhealthy and stinky, and it's a reversal that happened in an incredibly short time.

My girlfriend and I recently moved in together and we're talking about getting married. My problem is her fashion sense, which seems rooted sometime in the 1950s. I can't stand the way she dresses, and when we go out to parties or dinner, I'm embarrassed by the way people look at her. Am I putting style over substance here?

Be happy she has a fashion sense at all. Look at it this way: every decade's style eventually comes back in, so while you may think she's behind the times, she may actually be the trendsetter. Rather than focusing on how other people look at her, just consider it part of her personality. Some people want to fade into the woodwork when they're in public. Others prefer standing out like a Christmas tree ornament. This is part of who she is, and a part of what you liked about her in the first place. If you're talking about getting married, and she's perfectly wonderful in every other sense, ask yourself why some of the features that originally attracted you are now the same ones you'd like to change.

My boyfriend is older than me, and much more experienced in bed. When we have sex, I feel like I'm not giving him as much pleasure as he gives me, but I'm too embarrassed to ask him about it. How can I learn more about sex without cheating on him?

You probably wouldn't learn more about sex just by sleeping with someone else, anyway. After all, the parts are pretty much the same on any model you drive — it's only important how you handle the accessories.

I'd point you first in the direction of sexual literature. You might be surprised to find that even your suburban public library branch or bookstore can give you access to all kinds of books on sexuality, which is great. As for being embarrassed to ask him about it, try approaching the topic of what feels good for both of you when sex is not actually taking place. You'll probably find that easier than interrupting the flow in the middle with a "Hold it! I've got a question about what you're doing there!" Don't leave your notebook beside the bed, either.

I came home from work the other day and my wife said she had a surprise for me. The surprise turned out to be her best friend, in our bed. The three of us had sex together, and while it was a bit awkward at first, everything came out all right in the end. My problem is that the next day, after her friend went home, my wife confessed to me that the two of them have been having a lesbian affair for the last year. She told me she doesn't want to stop, but she also doesn't want to lose me, and we can continue having threesomes if I'll stay with her. I admit I enjoyed it as a one-time thing, but now I feel like she's paying me off with

group sex to excuse her cheating, and I don't think I like it. What should I do?

A Tell her you don't like it. Tell her you feel like you're being paid off. Tell her you're not for hire.

There are a few other issues here that you have not addressed. One is that she was doing something behind your back, and instead of telling you about it and asking for forgiveness, her way of dealing with it was to draw you into collusion instead. After all, now that you're an accessory after the fact to a sexual misdemeanor, how can you complain about the crime? It was the kind of nifty maneuver that is usually perpetrated only by heads of state, with the aid of vast undercover networks.

Basically, buddy, you've just been had. The message here is that if they've been having an affair for a year without you, they really don't need you. If the only way they can continue having the affair is to include you in the action, then once in a while they'll issue you the invitation, and pretend to have a good time. Doesn't this sound really attractive? Remember this is not a case of two women both lusting after your body. This is two women lusting after each other's bodies, and you happen to be the guy in the way.

No doubt your wife cares about you in other ways, so this may not be as difficult for her as it might be in other circumstances. Nevertheless, you have to question her inability to let you go while still staying involved with someone else. Most times when that happens, it's a case of someone hedging their bets: if one doesn't work out, there's always someone else around. I don't know about you, but I don't like being a consolation prize.

I would advise you to go off somewhere and seriously consider what it is you want; whether you feel this relationship is worth pursuing, changing, being in. No matter how you feel, do *not* think that just because they've put you in a compromising position, your options are now somehow limited. You can easily say what happened was a mistake, and is not the kind of thing you want to turn into a lifelong habit. No man likes to think he can be replaced by two vibrators.

My girlfriend has the most beautiful friends in the world, and they seem to all be hitting on me. They rub up against me at parties, and one of them has even come right out and asked me to come over to her apartment for "a coffee and some conversation some time." I'm young, I'm single, I'm male, I'm flattered as hell, and I'm afraid I might give in to temptation one night. What do I do?

Her girlfriends rub up against you because they find you safe. Your girlfriend has given you her stamp of approval, therefore you must be a good guy — not a serial killer or someone who does really disgusting things in bed. You are also accessible. They don't have to go out and find you because she already has. Because you're safe and available and present, they can try out their skills on you. Don't feel so flattered until you can walk into a party where no one knows you at all, and the beautiful women still all hit on you.

It seems to me that your real problem is that you find all these friends of your girlfriend so beautiful. Let's face it: they can't help being attractive, and something tells me that if they were a little more average-looking, you'd be asking me where you could find a very large flyswatter.

I'm going out with this guy and all he cares about is cars. His idea of a great day is talking about cars, fiddling with cars, and driving cars to car shows. How can I get him to broaden his interests, and who cares about an intercooled turbo charger anyway?

A I think you'd better change gears and try to get involved in some of his interests. There are many things you can do together in the car. Need I mention what they are? I'm sure even though he's mechanically inclined, he can think of things to do with his dipstick besides checking the oil. If this is his worst fault, and you love him, then it can't be all that bad. I won't suggest that you drape yourself naked over the car, but if you do, he'll probably notice your headlights.

Q My best friend slept with my boyfriend last night while I was at work. I know because today she phoned and told me. She says they were drunk, that she doesn't know what came over her, that she just asked him for a back rub and one thing led to another. She also says she's sorry, that it won't happen again. I haven't told my boyfriend I know yet, mainly because I'm not sure what to do. Help me!

A There are only two options here. The first is to forgive *and* forget. Someone famous once said forgiving without forgetting is like burying the hatchet with the handle sticking out — I agree. If the relationship is otherwise 24-karat and you are actually sincere, this may be a good approach. The second option is to look at this as a learning experience and put it, and them, behind you. You found out some pretty heavy information about both your friend and your boyfriend. This information classifies them either as fallible humans or as untrustworthy cads who deserve each other, and not you. Only you can decide which option to choose.

Q My boyfriend really likes X-rated movies, and although I'm not really offended by them, they don't seem to do much for me. Are there any out there that would be more satisfying for the both of us?

A There are erotic movies that have been written, directed, and produced by women. These usually differ from those created by men in that they tend to have a plot, and that the actual on-screen sex does not begin before the opening credits are even finished. Male-oriented videos most often center on a woman dragging the first man she sees off to bed, be he the pizza delivery boy or a door-to-door vacuum salesman. Either that, or they delve way too deeply into the dark side of violent sexual behavior. Videos created by women generally develop the relationships of their characters long before any sex takes place. Even when the sexual action does begin, it is usually not depicted in a series of microscopically gynecological close-up shots of genitals.

Basically, you're looking for something more erotic than anatomical, and you should be able to find it at your favorite video store. Try looking in the romance or drama sections, rather than behind the tattered curtain at the back of the store.

Q My husband is the only man I've ever slept with, and now I'm wondering if I've missed something. When I watch movies, I can't help thinking, "Gee, we don't kiss like that." Should I do something about it?

A People kissing on the screen have perfect lighting, makeup, and maybe even a decent script. It may look sexy and wonderful, but any actor will tell you it's much closer to lip gymnastics between strangers than a passionate moment between lovers.

Still, there is more to life, but so what? We're all missing something. There's always something great going on at a party to which we are not invited. If you're going to base the value of your life on the things you're *not* experiencing, you're always going to be disappointed. If your husband's kisses leave something to be desired, tell him, "You know, I really like to be kissed like this . . ." Then show him. Once he starts breathing again, he'll probably recognize the fun of learning a new skill.

When learning about sex, most teenagers spend about fifteen seconds in Hand-Holding 101, forty-five seconds at Kissing for Beginners, two minutes in Introduction to Necking, and then the rest of the semester attending as many classes as they can in Intercourse Made Easy. Of course, it's never too late to learn, and the homework can be a lot of fun.

Q **The last few women I've gone out with have been lousy kissers, to put it simply. It's like all of a sudden I'm kissing jaws instead of lips, or it feels like they're trying to swallow my face. What's going on here?**

A There are a lot of people out there who think bigger and wetter and wider is better. It's not. The idea seems to be that nothing but deep, French kissing will do, and it's an idea that's really overrated.

It's one thing if you're carried away in the moment; it's another thing entirely when it becomes the only method you know. In any kind of sexual activity, whether it's kissing or intercourse, doing the same thing over and over gets tiresome. Think of your sexual activity as a symphony: you go from a soft solo violin to a mad cacophony of drums and horns. The three most important points here are variety, variety, variety.

Usually when the action begins there is a kisser and a kissee. One person starts the smooch and generally sets the pace for how things are going to progress. If you're involved with someone whose technique is not to your liking, tell her to sit back and let you do the work, then move in and show her what you like. Most people seem to prefer kisses that are lighter, softer, and more provocative than the fast and furious, in-your-face style. The leave-you-breathless-wanting-more kind of kiss is probably more enjoyable than the type where someone is diving into your face.

Not enough people spend enough time learning good kissing techniques. It seems they all want to give you a quick peck and then head straight for the more exotic zones. Well, more exotic does not necessarily mean more erotic. You should not require a towel immediately afterward, and the subtlety of kissing is an art which should be studied more. For example, the *Kama Sutra* is one of the most famous publications on the topic of sex. It contains details of dozens of different kinds of kisses, and most of them include gentle contact with the lips closed.

I've been in a really good relationship for a long time, but sexually it's gotten really boring — the old missionary position. Every time I suggest we go back to the old adventurous days, he says we should settle down. By the way, we have a small child. What do you think?

Parenting has a big impact on every relationship. Just when you're getting down to the good stuff, in comes Junior with "Mommy, Mommy, why is the sky blue?" A small child can decimate your sex life, until you find a new rhythm for it. Remind your partner that with the baby asleep in the crib, you won't be interrupted while you enjoy yourselves in front of the fireplace, or on the kitchen table (okay, under the kitchen table).

As for settling down, you *are* settled down. You're stuck in the bedroom, in the bed, in the missionary position, with a small child down the hall. How much more settled down can anyone get? Get him out of the bedroom, flip him over, and have more fun somewhere else.

I just found my boyfriend's porno movies and I'm really upset at him. I once let him videotape us making love, and now I feel I'm competing against those girls. I feel cheap, and cheated. What should I do?

Get used to it. A lot of guys like porno movies. You may not like them in your house, but I don't think you should worry about competing with blue movie stars. I doubt your boyfriend is grading your performance on the X-scale. I'd suggest you hit the video store and try to find some more erotic (as opposed to pornographic) movies to bring home. Then perhaps you can get your boyfriend to see the romantic side to the physical act of making love. In the meantime, remember that the women you feel he's "cheating" with are made of celluloid. That said, make sure whatever it is you're doing, watching, or participating in is within your own limits of acceptability, not someone else's.

My boyfriend masturbates a lot, and he has a large collection of magazines like PLAYBOY and PENTHOUSE. Does this mean he's not satisfied with our sex life, or is he just oversexed?

A It's possible that it means neither. Men tend to be more aroused by visual stimuli than women are, which is why magazines like *Playboy* are so successful, and have been around for so long. Remember that a sex life is usually more than just intercourse. In fact, it includes more than the sum of your sexual activities. Your sex life is a combination of who you are and your life experiences. All of this influences what you bring to your lover in the way of desires, techniques, and much, much more. Adding fantasy to the mixture really doesn't mean more than that — fantasy. After all, he isn't taking Miss December to your mother's house for Christmas dinner.

Looking at lovely women isn't illegal (at least, not the last time I looked), and you really shouldn't read a raft of complicated possibilities into what is probably a very simple thing. His attraction to magazines is no measure of his satisfaction with your sex life together. Is there something wrong with him for having a large sex drive and liking the sight of naked women? No, I don't think he's oversexed. I think he's just a guy.

Q **I've got a problem that many guys have — my girlfriend loves lingerie and has dropped hints she wants some for her birthday. The one time I went into a lingerie store, I've never felt such fear and embarrassment in my life. Can you help me?**

A You could get her some lingerie from a mail-order catalog. If it's too late for that, save the idea for next year. That leaves two possible solutions. The first is to take a deep breath, close your eyes, and plunge into the store one more time, embarrassment be damned. The second is to get her something else this year (no, not power tools), and then tackle your phobia.

How? You could begin by taking a trip to the department store and walking through the area next to the lingerie section. Once that feels comfortable, make a pass through the lingerie section itself, without stopping — pretend you're on your way to men's wear and it just happened to be a good route. Next time, actually stop in the lingerie department and ask the clerk there for directions to the hardware area. Do it in gradual stages, and one day, you'll find yourself telling the clerk your girlfriend's size without even breaking a sweat.

My girlfriend spends a lot of time with her ex-husband. He sleeps over at her place, and she at his. Although she assures me she does not have a physical relationship with him, it still makes me uncomfortable. She says I'm insecure and old-fashioned, and don't trust her. Whose attitude needs adjusting here?

If he's so wonderful and they're sleeping at each other's homes, I'd be asking why they ever broke up! It sounds like she has the perfect relationship going. Unfortunately for you, you're only half of it.

I'm all for ex-spouses maintaining good relationships, especially when children are involved, but there's a long way between never speaking to your ex again and regular sleep-overs. Frankly, they're both a little old for pajama parties. Your girlfriend is unrealistic to think you should be celebrating this arrangement. Maybe you could suggest that the next time her ex needs a place to stay, your cousin Fred's couch is available.

My partner wants to have sex at least once a day. I'm happier doing the deed once a week. The rest of our relationship is just about perfect. How do we resolve our sexual differences?

A Sexual frequency in a relationship breaks down something like this: when both people are really turned on, it's the perfect opportunity to have sex. Not as good, but still acceptable, are those moments when one partner is really interested and the other is at least open to the possibility. Here, one person may have a fantastic time and the other at least a passable one. Then there are the times when one partner is really interested, and the other would rather be flossing their teeth. How do you resolve the impasse? The turned-on party could just take care of things by him/herself. If you're turned on, is it someone else's responsibility to satisfy you? I think a great deal of the responsibility for your pleasure lies with you.

There are other options, such as pretending to be interested. Surprisingly enough, pretending to be turned on often leads to *actually* being turned on. It's like someone talking you into a cruise, even though you aren't fond of boats, then you discover the voyage was fascinating. Maybe you aren't happy to start out on the trip, but you enjoy yourself once you get there.

Q I'm a city slicker, and my girlfriend is the outdoors type. To me, a day on the ski slopes should be followed by a night in front of the fire in a three-star hotel. She would rather cross-country ski through a glacier field and then sleep in a tent with a can of Sterno. How can we reconcile our different tastes?

A When two people have incredibly diverse interests, it can work out fine if both people are very independent. If both people like free time and have lots of friends to do things with, there's no conflict. On the other hand, if you're the type who likes to share all your activities with your partner, but you can't agree what those activities should be, you're going to run into trouble. Any healthy relationship should have room for both parties to have individual interests.

Be aware, though, that if *all* of your interests take you in opposite directions, and you have little time together, you may find yourselves becoming strangers. You'll discover your good experiences are all with others, so why are you in the relationship in the first place? The answer here, as so often, is balance and compromise. Some of the time, despite your distaste for campfires, go along (and don't bitch). Likewise, she can occasionally sit down with you in the lap of three-star luxury. That way, you'll both experience things you might not otherwise. More important, you've still have a relationship.

My girlfriend is pushing me to move in with her. She keeps saying it will be cheaper, we'll see more of each other, all that jazz. I'm not ready, but I'm afraid my outright refusal will break up an otherwise rockin' relationship. How do I keep from being ball-and-chained?

I guess you're *really* looking forward to sharing your life with another human being. Are you an only child? Do you have all your toys neatly lined up on the shelf where no one else can touch them? Some people find living with another person intolerable, because they're set on having their stuff "just so." If you do end up moving in together, perhaps you should try to find a two-bedroom apartment. That way, you can call the extra room the den, or whatever; you can still line up your CD collection any way you like (alphabetically, I bet); and you'll still feel like you have your own space.

That said, no one should ever get pushed into living with another person, either as lovers or roommates, and her arguments about convenience and economy are beside the point. What you have to decide is how committed you feel to your relationship. That is much more important to your decision than whether you want to share the shampoo.

Q **My girlfriend is really into the whole spandex routine, and I think it's sleazy. What do you think?**

A It's true that pouring certain body shapes into spandex should be a criminal offense. Since it is a free world, though, you might have to get used to the idea that what you consider too much, your girlfriend considers just right.

Many people like spandex for its elastic properties — it helps keep the jiggle to a minimum. This probably makes it ideal for dance routines, aerobic classics, and cycling. Assuming your girlfriend isn't wearing it to wedding receptions or business meetings, your only option is to tell her how you feel. Be prepared for a rocky reception, though. Few women appreciate being told how to dress, unless your last name happens to be Armani.

Q **My boyfriend and I have been together for two years, we have a baby, we have good jobs, and everything is going great. The only problem is that we aren't married, and it really bothers me, even though I believe we are together for life. How do I bring up the subject without proposing to him?**

A You're intimate enough to live together and raise a child together and talk about your future together, and the one thing you can't talk about is whether you'll get married? It seems to me you've already discussed subjects much more intricate, involved, and serious than buying a license and saying "I do." If you don't want to propose yourself (and there's nothing wrong with a woman proposing), then at least you can open up a discussion about what marriage means to you, versus what it means to him. At this point, you really don't know whether he wants to get married or not. Since you're concerned about it, it's probably a good time to find out how he feels.

The only thing stopping me from proposing to my girlfriend is oral sex — I love it, she thinks it's immoral and dirty. Should I forget that part of my sex life and ask her to marry me anyway?

Probably not. If something's getting in the way of thinking that you could live with this woman for the rest of your life, then you owe the subject some serious inspection. It's unlikely that she's going to change her position, but it's worth a try. Remember, though, that people only change their view on something if they have reason to do so, and your pleading and cajoling after getting married is not going to be a good enough reason for her.

True, you can decide that because of all her other sterling qualities, the lack of oral sex is something with which you're prepared to live. Or you can decide that sex in all its variety includes oral sex, and you simply can't see yourself sharing your life with someone who considers this part of sex immoral and dirty. Better to realize that now than after you're married.

Q Why do women always want to change men? You get into what looks like a good relationship, and then all of a sudden she hates this and that about you and wants you to change.

A For the most part, women have been socialized to be nurturing and helpful, to fix broken things, to clean up messes. Many women take this outlook and impose it on men — with a little redecorating and renovating and fixing up, a little shining and polishing, this guy would be just fine. There's another factor at work here as well. When people first get involved, the incredible romantic and sexual attraction leads them to disregard any faults they each might have, to see each other in a very idealized form. As the initial haze wears off, they begin to notice each other's blemishes, and some people are unprepared for the revelation. It's also true that at the start of a relationship, people pretend to be better adjusted, more accepting, open, and adventurous than they really are. The way around this is to keep the lines of communication open. Keep talking, don't pretend to be someone you aren't, and don't say you can accept a character trait that you actually consider to be a fatal flaw.

Q When I met my boyfriend, I quickly discovered he had a virginity thing, so I let him believe he was the first. Now we've been together two years and we're talking about marriage, but I feel guilty about this one untruth in our relationship. I've never lied to him about anything else. Should I tell him about the one time I did?

A Most of the time in relationships (and just about everywhere else), lying is not a very good idea. However, sometimes not telling the entire truth is not only okay, it's advisable. In your case, unless a guy you once had sex with is about to arrive on your doorstep and announce it to your boyfriend, I'd suggest you let it go. Leave your boyfriend with the idea that he was the first. What difference does it really make whether you did some heavy fooling around before you met him, or if there were actual genitals involved? If you ever find yourself confronted about this part of your past, you can always say, with conviction, that although he may not have been the first man with whom you had sex, he was the first man with whom you made love.

Q I met a really neat woman a few months ago and we've been going out ever since. The problem is that every time we get close to having sex (and I mean close!), she backs off. We're both single, over twenty-one, non-virgins, and have safety in mind (read: condoms), so I don't understand what's going on here. I respect a woman's decision, so I always stop when she says no. But after so many aborted takeoffs, I can't help wondering if maybe she prefers her men to be a bit more aggressive. What should I do?

A Don't get aggressive. For openers, try telling her this: "I'm finding this really difficult, getting so close and then backing off, without understanding what's going on. So the only solution I can think of is to not do anything at all until you're ready, in which case you can let me know." Put the ball in her court. Let her come to you when the time is right for her.

Q My husband and I have been married for six years now, and we're coming up on another anniversary soon. Some of my friends say all men have affairs when they've been married this long. Does the seven-year itch really exist?

A Some people believe that we're predestined to seek change in our lives every seven to ten years. Even if you subscribe to this belief, though, it doesn't necessarily mean the change involves a new sexual partner. It could be a new career, having children, or moving to another country, just to name three. I don't think your partner (or anyone else's) is going to run out and have an affair simply because he's been married for seven years. There are people who have been married for forty or fifty years without feeling the need to cheat on their spouses. And there are probably millions more who have felt the itch without scratching.

Do people look around and wonder how their relationship is doing after a lengthy period of time with the same partner? Yes. The conclusion many come to, however, is that their relationship may need changes, or their own life may need changes, but not in the area of sneaking around on their mate.

Q I've been married for two years to a woman I thought was heaven sent. A recent argument resulted in her confessing that she was seeing another guy for the first month of our relationship, and also had sex with another guy a year later at Christmas while I was out of town. I've also been away at numerous other times and couldn't get hold of her. Now she says she's sorry, that she was messed up, but to know she was sleeping with two guys (that I know of) makes my heart sink. What do I do? I love her, but is she who she says she is?

A Confession may calm her soul and unburden her mind, but hey, what a coincidence, now yours weighs an extra ton. How giving of her. It's possible she's risking her happiness and her relationship with you because of some prior life experiences. She may be sabotaging herself, and the only way out I know for her is counseling.

In the meantime, you sound like you're questioning whether her confession has been total or partial, but you also seem to have an open mind toward the continuation of this relationship. Your own answer might be to go to counseling with her, so you can both get the answers you need.

Q **Some of my ex-boyfriends have cheated on me, and I was completely oblivious about it until either a friend told me, or I literally caught them in the act. Now I'm in a new relationship, and I'm a little worried about it. Is there any surefire way to tell whether your boyfriend is faithful?**

A Let's start with the four behavior changes about which *Monogamy Myth* author Peggy Vaughan warns: (1) Changes in attention — has he become more aloof? Is he less attentive than he once was? (2) Sexual changes — is he more or less interested in sex than before? (3) Aesthetic changes — is he suddenly concerned about his weight or thinning hair? Has he recently joined a gym after years of inactivity? If he always seems to be buying new underwear, be suspicious. (4) Schedule changes — is he suddenly required to be away from home more often, or has he begun taking a lot more business trips without you?

Be aware here that like many illness symptoms, these signs can mean more than one thing (like a life crisis, for instance). It's entirely possible for him to have all four and still be faithful. If you're at the place where you suspect he's cheating, talk about it with him. Sitting silently in the corner eating pounds of comfort food is not going to resolve your misgivings. Instead, sit down together, tell him what you've been noticing, and ask if there's anything going on that you need to talk about.

Our youngest daughter has just left home for college. This means that after eighteen years of closing the door to the bedroom and being quiet, my husband and I can finally once again make love whenever, wherever, and as noisily as we like. Unfortunately, after eighteen years of closing the door, etc., we seem to be stuck in a rut, and the rut is in the middle of our king-size bed. Can you recommend some other locations around the house that don't require the physique of a teenager? (We're both too old for hanging off the chandelier.)

Any room with a cushioned floor, a heated floor, or lots of great things on which you can flop around should fill your bill. Some people find the room least likely to be used for sex becomes the biggest turn-on. Bedrooms are fairly predictable, which is why many people explore the nooks and crannies elsewhere. You may find the idea of having sex in a broom closet ludicrous, but other people will put it number one on their list of locations. Kitchens are great for cooking up romance as well — there are lots of toys, things to rub up against, things that put out heat of their own. If you need a time out, snacks are readily available, and things like the whipping cream in the fridge can be put to a variety of uses. As always, imagination makes for the best recipe, regardless of which corner of the house you find erotic.

Q I'm probably an average woman of my age when it comes to my sexual experience, but I'm a little lacking in one area. How can I say this? I want to learn how to give better oral sex. Can you recommend a book on the subject?

A I don't know of an instructional book specifically dealing with oral sex, but there are chapters on the subject in many other books about sexuality. You might want to spend a few minutes in a bookstore or your library's Human Sexuality department. As far as oral sex goes, technique rates third, after letting your imagination run loose, and an enthusiastic and open approach.

In any intimate sexual relationship, it's vital to know whether your partner is enjoying what's going on. Therefore, you need to communicate, either verbally or through gestures, since neither of you can read the other's mind. If talking about it seems too difficult, ask your partner to moan louder when it feels better. Then pretend you're a scientist and start experimenting. I'm sure your partner will be delighted to take part in your research project.

Q Why don't men buy magazines like COSMO, ELLE, and VOGUE, the kind of magazines that tell women how to have relationships? Aren't men interested in improving their relationships with women?

A There actually are some men's magazines with articles on relationships. Still, by and large, you're right. You don't see many magazines with headlines like "Be Muscle Confident — Use Those Pecs with Flair" or "How I Got Maria to Marry Me, by Arnold Schwarzenegger" or "Are You Still Waiting for Ms. Perfect?" Men's and women's magazines have some intrinsic differences that would require a five-year in-depth study to resolve, and maybe not even then. Myself, if I were a man, I'd probably be reading the women's magazines — it's one way to find out what's lurking inside the female mind. Unfortunately, most men buy only men's magazines, which aim at relationships more from a problem-solving angle — as in "How do I get her to stay overnight even though I'm watching the football game?" — rather than a relationship angle — as in "How can I tell if she's just using me?"

What does it mean when a man with whom you have had a monogamous relationship for seven years suddenly wants to wear condoms? He claims he only recently found out the incubation period for AIDS can be ten years or more.

I'd be checking his pockets for a few other things besides condoms, like matches from singles bars or keys from motels out on the highway. Usually if someone has a sudden change in sexual behavior, it's a signal that perhaps something else is going on. The idea of the incubation period for AIDS being longer than was first thought has been around for quite a long time. Either he's suddenly become very paranoid about the issue, or he now wants to keep his unit gift-wrapped because he's been sharing it with someone other than you. Also, if his sudden desire to wear condoms is accompanied by a new membership at a fitness club, a change in hair style, and a sudden yen to trade in his four-door sedan for a convertible sports car, *then* I'd be very suspicious.

Remember one thing, though: you really don't know yet whether it's paranoia or guilt or something else entirely. Don't jump to conclusions until you check things out further.

Q My husband and I are former national team athletes. We have a great relationship and used to have a terrific sex life. Since retiring from competition and losing a bit of the old athlete's tone, we both seem to have become a little self-conscious in bed, and it's affecting our enjoyment. Any ideas?

A Either you like how you look, or you don't. For many women in particular, five or ten pounds can really put the brakes on a sex drive. Women think, "How can I possibly have good sex when I have to take my clothes off and expose those extra pounds?" Guys, on the other hand, tend to regard extra pounds as more to love.

It sounds to me like your problem is you have greater expectations of yourselves because you were athletes, and therefore used to be above-average in the fitness department. You can either lower your expectations and make friends with the bodies you now have, or do something to regain your lost tone. One possibility would be to start a new aerobics regimen together.

In the meantime, turn off the lights and light some candles. Everything looks great in candlelight, and you won't notice your few extra pounds as much if you dim the glare of the overhead bulbs.

Disconnecting

In the beginning, there's promise. In the middle, there's activity and history. In the end, there's just dividing up the cutlery and deciding who gets the cat. The end of a relationship is never any fun, and the best you can hope for is that it will be a relief when the process is completely, and finally, over.

There is no joy in parting for the majority of us. As a species, we're not really that good at it. We don't deal with death very well, and we don't deal with separations very well, either. As a result, people come up with techniques to get out of relationships by the side door, instead of heading out the main exit, head held high.

The first of these methods is the *Slam the Door* technique. Although you've had a wonderful relationship, it's over, and you can't stand the idea that you're not going to be together any more. So you set up a situation where one person can hate the other, leaving with the big bang instead of the long whimper. This is a common technique. It basically explains why a couple can seem wonderfully happy and terribly in love one day, then run around bad-mouthing each other the next.

The second common way of obliquely ending a relationship is something I call the *Catapult* technique. This happens most often when one person realizes the relationship is over, but they still really like their soon-to-be ex-partner, and feel sorry for them. That person then finds a situation that will catapult them out of the relationship — something big enough to leave no room for second tries. This usually works out to be a new partner ("I'm leaving you for something better") or the consolation prize ("I'm leaving you but I'll still be your friend"). Unfortunately, this rarely works for either party. Jumping from one relationship to another — the rebound — is rarely a successful life strategy. It's always best when a relationship is over to get out of it *before* you start up a new one. Sometimes the desire for a new lover is just an indicator that you've come to the end of the line with the old one.

As for turning lovers into just friends, let's just say that the person left behind in pain doesn't want to see your face every five minutes as a "friend" when they're actually lusting after your body.

Breaking up is a separation of people, and a separation of the accoutrements of a life spent together. It may be difficult to decide who gets the lead crystal or the big-screen TV, but those choices are a snap compared with who gets the family members. If the list includes only budgies and a cocker spaniel, it's hard. If the list begins with sons and daughters, it's agonizing. Where will Bobby and Susie be best off? If the ex-partners are going to live in separate cities or countries, how will they keep up the relationships with their children, now so far away? The legal systems of most democratic countries are clogged to overflowing trying to resolve these dilemmas, because so many times, the people involved can't seem to do it on their own.

It's been said that people who are parting should leave each other in one piece. Because you honor and respect the great relationship you once had, end it as gently and kindly and ethically as possible. In an ideal world, this would happen every time. Being the flawed human beings we all are, it unfortunately happens much less often.

How do you get an ex to let go and go away? Two years after breaking up, she still calls me every other week. Sometimes it's a tearful "I love you," and sometimes it's screaming and threats. What do I do?

The first thing you can do is stop taking all her calls. The unfortunate thing about the telephone is that the person who makes the call is obviously ready to do business, while the person who answers has no advance warning what kind of transaction is about to begin. Taking control of this interchange means screening calls before you pick up. That means either buying an answering machine or signing up for a call-display service with your phone company.

Once you're in a position to accept her calls only when you're ready for them, you're ready to deal with the larger issue. You can suggest to her that if she's still glued to you, two years after your relationship ended, then perhaps it's time she talked to someone about it. Tell her she needs to be getting on with her life, since that's what you are doing with yours. Let her know that you wish her well and have fond feelings for the time you had together, but that it really and truly is over. Try to make her understand there's no chance things are ever going to begin again. If you accept a tearful "I love you," you may be leaving her the wrong impression. She may conclude that if she calls and badgers you often and long and hard enough, she may wear you down to the point where you will be available again.

Phoned-in screams and threats are illegal in most places, and scary in all. With these, I think you must tell her where your limits are, and then you must follow through. If you say you won't take any more calls, and then let her phone you, she'll know your limits are bogus.

If you know any of her friends or family well, you might call and ask them to help with the situation by speaking with her. One thing is certain: you cannot be a counselor to an ex-boyfriend or ex-girlfriend.

 How do you mend a broken heart?

One-word answer, and probably the last word you want to hear: time. Somewhere down the line, it's likely you will barely remember the name of the one who left you wounded. It is okay to be sad and depressed, and in fact you should be. If this person actually meant something, you can hardly be expected to forget them over a long weekend.

Part of what you're going through is the unwinding of the relationship. The same way it takes time to get one going, it takes time to wind one down. Give yourself permission to cry, to feel bad. Take a lot of bubble baths. Get in the hot tub. Treat yourself. Buy something you've always wanted, like that new CD player, and add a box of chocolates to the order. Believe it or not, chocolate triggers the release of the same chemical in the body that is created when we fall in love. That probably goes a long way in explaining how gifts of chocolate became associated with romance in the first place.

I went out with this guy and he seemed really nice in the beginning, but now he just wants to be with me constantly. He phones all the time and I don't have the heart to get rid of him, because I feel sorry for him. I feel trapped, and I shudder every time the phone rings. What should I do?

A It's the last half of the last decade of the millennium, and you're going to tell me you don't own an answering machine? Come on, girl, get one. That's step one.

Step two is more difficult, but necessary. Dating someone because you feel sorry for them is the ultimate put-down. The message you're sending is that this is the best deal he'll ever get — dating someone who doesn't want him. Free the guy up and let him find someone else. And remember, when the phone rings, as Ogden Nash once said, "If called by a panther, don't anther."

I'm now a single mother of two, as the man I've been with for eight years has chosen to push us aside for work and a little affair. Lately he's come around being nice to me when he wants something, and like a fool I give in. Other times he treats me like hell and demands to take the children. Please help me.

A After eight years, you seem to now believe your ex is the only man on the planet. He is certainly not treating you like *you're* one in a billion. After so long with this one man, you may have forgotten what it's like to have someone treat you well. You can't avoid all interaction with him as the father of your children, but you shouldn't let him bully or cajole you into sleeping with him, either. The only relationship you owe him is with his kids, not with you. Whatever contact he does have with you should be civil, and if he seems incapable of treating you with respect, I'd suggest you have someone else with you when he comes to see the children. Some people seem to display their best behavior only in front of an audience.

In the meantime, work on yourself. You certainly deserve more than what you're getting from this man, and you certainly don't owe him a physical relationship because of past favors.

Q **I've been in love with my ex since the day we met in '93, but we recently split up and are now fighting over child custody. My problem is I can't stop thinking about her. Each day we're apart I love her more, and it hurts more. I want to get back together. She says "Maybe." Why can't I let go?**

A I think the two of you should go for family counseling, regardless of whether you're going to reconcile. You can call it marriage counseling, couples counseling, or separation counseling, but the process is still the same: two people sitting down with a third party, trying to figure out what went wrong. Your goal will be either to fix the problems, or to have some understanding of them, so you can avoid the pitfalls in your next relationships.

Since you have children, you'll be seeing each other for about the next twenty years, one way or the other. It is therefore in both your best interests to put together the most friendly relationship you can. Part of the reason you can't let go is that you still aren't sure which way you're going, and family counseling will help with that as well. Just don't make yourself her doormat to walk over, while you're sorting out your past, present, and future feelings.

Q **My girlfriend and I broke up quite a while ago and I haven't seen her since. Even though we weren't great together, I don't see why our friendship has to die with the closer relationship. Should I call her?**

A First ask yourself: what qualities does she have that would make her a good friend? If you can list them for yourself, and they don't come down to mere nostalgia for the good times of your past relationship, then by all means put her on your Possible Friends list and give her a call. If, on the other hand, you still have unresolved feelings about your past relationship, seeing her regularly as a friend may reopen wounds not properly healed yet.

It's very difficult for anyone to go from lovers mode to friends mode without some intervening time. If enough time has passed for you to no longer be burdened by old baggage, then the transition may work. If you're still wondering why you broke up and how it might have been different, then I'd suggest you go shopping for friends in another market.

My boyfriend and I just broke up, and he owes me a lot of money. When I lent it to him, things were going great and we were happy, but our breakup was really nasty and now we're not on speaking terms. Will I ever see my money again?

No, probably not. If you aren't even on speaking terms, it's highly unlikely he's going to square up a debt he incurred when things were peachy. What you can do is try sending him a request for payment in writing. Detail what you feel the arrangement was, and how he can start repaying what he owes, but don't hold your breath waiting for a check. If the amount was reasonably small, I'd say write it off to a lesson learned. Since you say it was a lot, you could try getting a lawyer involved. Even oral contracts are legally binding. They're just harder to prove unless you have witnesses to the original transaction.

When lending money — whether it's to boyfriends, girlfriends, cousins, aunts, uncles, or next-door neighbors — always put it in writing. Even when people love each other truly and deeply, they sometimes misunderstand the terms of the deal when they're using someone else's cash. Putting the whole thing down on paper saves a lot of grief down the line.

It won't guarantee you'll get your money back, but it will make the possibility considerably greater.

If you feel uncomfortable drawing up contracts with your significant other, you might try blaming the whole thing on a third party. Tell him/her that your lawyer/accountant/financial advisor/guru *insists* you get it in writing, and you're really embarrassed to be asking, but you always do what your financial planner tells you to do, blah, blah, blah . . . Making someone else the bad guy (even a fictitious someone else) and then apologizing for it can ease your discomfort, get him to sign the agreement, and leave both sides satisfied with the bargain. The truth is, when money is involved, there are just too many places for errors, misunderstandings, and heartache, even when both parties are honest and have only the best intentions.

After four years with my girlfriend, we became engaged. I thought our relationship was perfect. One day, she comes over, hands back my ring, and says, "Sorry, I love you as a friend, we've just grown apart." Now my world is shattered, not because a relationship didn't work out but because I feel like I was a fool who was obviously living a fantasy. Should I have done something differently?

You are not a fool. You had a perfectly wonderful time in this relationship. You had fantasies and dreams, lots of making out, probably some good kissing occurred — it wasn't exactly a total loss. As changeable as feelings are, they don't come with an ironclad guarantee. At least your girlfriend was honest with you. She let you know that as far as she's concerned, the breakup wasn't due to anything you did, and that as a person, you are still quality material.

A relationship is always made up of three parties. There's you, there's her, and there's "the relationship." The relationship has a personality of its own, and sometimes it just gets to be this unfriendly presence of which no one wants to be a part. It has nothing to do with either of the people involved; it's just that the relationship itself is an unwanted party.

As unhappy as you are with your world falling apart, don't feel foolish. Love is a powerful and overwhelming emotion. When you look back on this relationship, don't dwell on its end. Instead, think of the highlights, the wonderful times you wouldn't have had if the connection had never existed. I believe I am a part of all I have met. If you accept that, you will understand that you could not be the fine, upstanding person you are now if you had never met your ex-fiancée. Your next relationship will be the better for it.

My boyfriend of four years woke up yesterday and told me that he was no longer in love with me. I am devastated and humiliated. We did everything together and I thought he was happy. How can a person be so close to you one minute and then fall out of love in the next breath? Did he ever love me?

If we could patent a device for falling in love and staying that way, we'd probably be on the brink of world peace. Falling is the easy part. It's the staying in love that is so much more difficult.

I don't think you should deny the past and torture yourself by wondering if there ever was love there — assume there was. Perhaps he has been unable to express his feelings until this point. Many men do not process their thoughts out loud, but instead do it internally and then announce the conclusion. You are the same wonderful person you were before meeting him. The only part that failed was the relationship, not you.

Q I'm a thirty-seven-year-old single mother of two who's in love with a man seventeen years my senior. He is married with two sons, and no, I'm not waiting for him to leave his wife. He's always been honest with me, and has always said that while he loves me, he would never leave his wife and family. My problem is that I'm very happy when I'm with him, but still very confused as well. I guess I'm looking more for prediction than advice. Where do you think this is going?

A I think this is going nowhere. You're dating a man who's pushing fifty-five years old, and who is not going to leave his wife. Considering his age, my guess is his kids are adults by now. That means the "family" he won't leave is his wife, period. The situation as it stands is just great for him. He has his wife, whom he loves, and he has this hot affair going with a thirty-seven-year-old single mother.

I have to wonder if things are so sunny for you. You have a family of your own — don't you want someone to share at least some of the unique moments of your life with your kids, even if it's not their own father? My guess is that this arrangement works much better for him than for you, and your confusion is just your mind's way of covering up the fact that you have to make a decision. Keep in mind that as long as you're involved with someone who is unavailable, *you* are unavailable to have a relationship with someone who might better fit your life.

Q I'm having an affair with a married man. He keeps saying he's going to leave his wife, but he's been saying that for a long time with no action. We have a great relationship, but I'm starting to wonder what I should do about the future.

A First, a rash generalization that holds true oh-so-often: married men never leave their wives. Okay, almost never. If you are looking for a very limited relationship, this will probably work for you. It means you must be satisfied spending Valentine's Day, his birthday, and most holidays like Christmas on your own, because his obligations on those days will be to his family, and not to you. In fact, if you're happy with these limitations, you'd probably also do well being married to a doctor or a lawyer. The only difference is that in those cases, it will be patients and clients who will take up his time, and not another woman.

Having an affair with a married man is like being involved with someone who lives on another continent. If it's important to you to be able to come and go as you please, without having to answer to anyone, then a married man is for you.

Q **A couple in my neighborhood have been casual friends of mine for about a year now, and I recently became lovers with the woman. We didn't plan for it to happen, and now we're stuck for a way to tell her boyfriend, as neither of us wants to hurt his feelings, but we don't want to continue deceiving him either.**

A You should remind your woman friend that she is in a relationship right now, and it isn't with you. If her current connection isn't working and she wants to make a change, then she should, and you can tell her you could be available when she does. Right now, you're the third party, and a convenient one for her. What you may find out is that even if she leaves her boyfriend, you may be only a short-term rebound on the way to the rest of her life. Personally I've always believed that if you have a dead relationship on your hands, you should bury it before you go looking for a live one.

Family
and Friends

We are both the beneficiaries and the victims of our family experiences, because your first exposure to anything will always be significant. This is true whether it's spying your first spider in the basement, or watching your first sunset at the beach. As you can imagine, your exposure to the relationships within your family will have an enormous impact on how you look at other people in your later life, and how you interact with them.

Academics love jargon, and they've come up with the term "undifferentiated family ego mass" to describe how family dynamics typically work. The idea is that a family is more than a collection of older and younger people: it actually has a life of its own. The individual members of the family will have different roles and responsibilities within it, just as the many employees of a large corporation have their roles and responsibilities. Unlike the cogs in corporate wheels, however, members of healthy families are allowed to switch roles. At different times, you may be the "good guy" or the "brat," and as long as you don't get stuck playing one part, everything will be fine.

Unfortunately, many people grow up in families where the opportunities aren't so varied. They end up with lessons not learned, and developmental levels not passed. As a result, when they pack their clothes to go off into the world outside the family, they end up also packing the emotional baggage of unfinished business, and they carry that baggage with them into their new relationships.

The people we pick as friends mark our first attempts to broaden our tribe by including people who don't share our genetic makeup. It's also our first grab at independence since, as my own mother is fond of saying, you can pick your friends, but you can't pick your relatives.

Unfortunately, some people choose friends they'd probably be better off having as enemies. It happens when we fail to first consider the traits we'd be happy with in a friend, or even an acquaintance. It's nice to have friends who actually like you, people who think you're wonderful and are supportive, but still have the honesty to let you know when they think you're going off track. When we're lucky, we find friends who last a lifetime. When we're unlucky, we find friends who barely last a lunchtime. Between the two extremes come the people who pass through our lives, hopefully leaving memories and lessons learned. Not all friendships are forever, but that's not necessarily a tragedy, despite how it may feel when a great relationship reaches its end.

There are no exams or grades in Life 101, so many of us fumble our way through relationships, never knowing why some worked well and others failed miserably. It doesn't mean all our future connections will be cursed, but it means more catch-up time to learn the lessons missed at home.

I'm a thirty-year-old woman, gay, and attached — these are not my problems. My problems are my two children, who I feel

are too young to understand my love life. My oldest (she's eight) recently caught my partner and me sleeping together, so I told her we just fell asleep watching TV in my room, and are really good friends. The incident has me wondering when I should tell my kids about my lifestyle, and <u>how</u> I should tell them about it. Also, I'm my mom's youngest, and I haven't told her either, for fear of hurting her.

A Your children are probably *not* too young to understand your love life. Children understand whether people care about each other or not. It seems obvious you have someone in your life that you care about, and who cares about you. It's important that your kids know that, as most children certainly get to see enough people who are angry or upset or disappointed with each other, or who are just plain enemies. People should never be embarrassed about good feelings, especially feelings of love.

As for how to tell your children, you do it in much the same way you convey other sensitive information: give it to them at their own age level. You probably shouldn't tell an eight-year-old the intimate details of your sex life, regardless of whether your sexual partner is of the opposite gender or the same. What you can explain to your daughter is that some women have partners who are men, and some women have partners or special friends who are other women.

Obviously, you can't avoid explaining things to your children forever. When it comes to your mother, however, what you do and when you do it depend on how much of your lifestyle you want to share with her. There is no formula for this, and you do not owe anyone information about whether you are or are not gay. Some people find keeping their sexual preference at a distance from their parents works well. Others say that creates a situation in which their parents don't know who they are.

If you can't make up your mind which way to go, try getting in touch with PFLAG (Parents and Friends of Lesbians and Gays). They won't be able to decide for you, but they can give you the benefit of knowing how others in your situation have handled the issue.

Should parents let their children have sex at home?

 No. Kids should sneak around. Really, I'm serious. Your sex life is important stuff, and it should be private. If you can't afford a place for sex, odds are you're too young to be doing it in the first place. Here's a hint: Ever heard of a tent? Go camping!

 Do my parents still have sex? If so, how often?

 Yes, and probably often enough to make you uncomfortable about it, too. Why are we all so weirded out by the idea of our parents having sex? We all come from a long line of people who had sex. Let's face it, if they hadn't, we wouldn't be here. As far as their frequency goes, many things probably get in the way of increasing it. These include having to worry about retirement plans, how to pay for vacations, where to get the money for that new car, trying to pay off the mortgage early, and how to still leave some money for *us* in their wills. See — don't you feel guilty now?

 My boyfriend and I had unprotected sex while we were drunk at a party, and now I think I might be pregnant. When my parents find out, I'm afraid that they'll go berserk and disown me. How can I tell them?

A If you think telling your parents is the difficult part, think again. Think about devoting the next twenty years of your life to bringing up a child. Consider a couple of thousand diaper changes, trips to the hospital, visits with the teachers, paying for braces. Think about worrying that your little bundle of joy will get drunk at a party and either create or become a teenage mom. As a matter or fact, consider that conceiving while drunk is probably not the best way to begin life as a parent in the first place.

Once you're done contemplating all that, realize that if the pregnancy continues, then you have my ironclad guarantee your parents are going to find out. It's just physically impossible to hide it forever. With that in mind, the sooner you tell your parents, the better. If, on the other hand, you decide to have an abortion, then it is entirely up to you whether you ever share the information with your parents. The decision to end a pregnancy is strictly your own.

Q **I'm currently seeing a guy who has a record, and I don't mean music. My parents found out when he was foolish enough to admit it to them. They waited until he left and then went nuts on me. What happened in his past was a mistake, but my parents — forget it! What do I do?**

A While it was naive on his part to casually admit to a criminal record, I have a hard time understanding your parents' apparent interviewing techniques for prospective sons-in-law. ("Do you have a record? Have you ever been in jail? Are you a member of a cult, a militia, or a book-of-the-month club?") It's unfortunate that your boyfriend owned up to his past before your parents got to know what a wonderful guy he turned out to be. Since the record is out of the bag, you'll probably just have to let time erase the black mark. His good nature and love for you will become apparent to your family as they get to know him. Hopefully, your parents will grow to view him as you do — or, if not, at least to accept him honestly.

Q **My mom was dating this guy, he has a son who I really like, and we've dated. Now, my mom and his dad have gotten married. Can we still date?**

A If you're still living at home under your parents' roof, I'd say no, it's a bad idea. You're not related by blood, but you are now related by marriage, and family relationships are complicated enough without dating your new stepbrother.

If you are all grown up, living away from home, you think this guy is the last great romance of your life and you just couldn't possibly live without him, then you can continue dating him, but keep the risks very much in mind. A blended family is still a family. If you continue your relationship and it ends badly, how will you face the prospect of family dinners together, the holidays, and all the rest? The best thing about an ex-boyfriend or ex-girlfriend is that you don't have to see them any more. When your ex is a member of the family, you don't have that option.

Q **My family is screwed up, and I'm no exception. At the age of twenty, I was in a happy relationship, but I ended it once I learned my family members disapproved. Two years later, I find myself re-examining the unresolved feelings left by the quick breakup. In fact, I still love him. Should I ask him how he feels, or**

forget about him and move on? I'd like to be with him, but as you can tell, I still can't make my own decisions.

My Auntie Bea once said this to me: "You'll know you're all grown up when you no longer need your parents' approval." There are definite family patterns, but don't feel as though your future relationships will be exactly like those in your family. You have the option of taking the benefits you found there and working through the drawbacks. If you still love somebody, remember that it's you who have to kiss him, not your mom and dad. If you still want to be with him, take the risk and call him. You'll never know what could have been if you don't.

I'm nineteen years old and have a problem with my mother. She and I are best friends until I become involved with a man, then all we do is fight. I can't sleep over at my boyfriend's house without her calling me names the next morning. Sometimes it gets so bad I'm forced to end a perfectly fine relationship just to shut her up. I'm very responsible, and besides going to school I also work full-time. How do I stop her running my life?

I'd guess that your mom is single and/or you are the last to leave home — the empty-nest syndrome is common for parents at those times in their lives. If you graduate, find a boyfriend, and move out, your mother loses her full-time job: mothering you. I'd say the best way to get her to stop running your life is to help her get involved in her own. If she packed in her university career to become a full-time mother, remind her how much time she now has to go back and get that degree, since she no longer has to tend to you all day. Bring home some travel brochures on that trip she's always wanted to take. Give her some subtle reminders that her job as a parent includes eventually kicking you out of the nest, and that your test flights seem to be checking out just fine.

I took my five-year-old son over to a friend's house the other day. While playing in the backyard, their five-year-old daughter pulled my son into a shed, kissed him, and pulled down his pants. He was quite upset for a while. Is this normal for kids that young?

Young children may not be sexually active, but they are sexually curious, so yes, it is normal behavior, however disturbing it may be to parents. Our society expects that there be no dress rehearsal for relationships. We are supposed to keep our genitals under wraps until we find our lifelong partner, then get the whole thing right in one shot. The truth is that children are curious. This little girl may have been more aggressive than most, but the old "You show me yours, I'll show you mine" is common among kids, and I doubt your little boy has been emotionally scarred by the event. Nonetheless, it's probably a good time to explain to your son that he has the right to say no to anyone who wants to look at or touch his privates, including his friends.

Be careful that you don't sabotage your future relationship with your son by reacting too strongly to this kind of news. It's important not to let your own apprehensions or anxieties take over. Children pick up their parents' adverse reactions very quickly. If they decide that a certain topic upsets Mommy or Daddy too much, they'll quickly stop asking those types of questions. When a five-year-old brings you his or her first sex story ("Mommy, I was showing Billy mine and he was showing me his, and I saw . . ."), and you keel over in shock and disgust, you may be causing the very trauma in your child that you were worried about in the first place.

Q **I'm twenty years old, and my boyfriend has asked me to move in with him. My problem is that he lives a couple of thousand miles away. I've been accepted into a university there, so it's not really the distance, but my parents would have a fit if they knew I was going to be living with him, and not in a dorm. What should I do?**

A Down through the centuries, there's one method that's been used by people to avoid big scenes with their parents: you can lie to them. You can be vague about your living arrangements. Let your parents believe you're going to be living in the dorm, then move in with your boyfriend. Get a good answering machine, and be sure he never answers the phone. The technique is commonly called "sneaking around." You never know — your parents may have used it on *their* parents.

At twenty, I think you have to choose your own living arrangements. Your parents may have a fit, but they have each other, and their own lives to run. Your job now is to figure out your own values. If you feel good about moving in with your boyfriend, it's your decision and your right. In that case, you have to be able to say, "Look, I know you're really upset about my choice, and I've taken your point of view into account, but this is my decision now. This is really what I want to do. I hope you'll bear with me and still be a big part of my life."

I think the healthiest families are those able to incorporate more than one point of view, whether on politics, religion, or the kids' relationships. Just about everyone does things of which their parents disapprove. What you have to ask is whether *you* approve of moving in with your boyfriend, whether it's right at this time in your life. The consequences of your actions are yours to enjoy or survive. So the decision has to be yours as well.

I'm eighteen and my girlfriend is seventeen. My problem is that her mother is incredibly overprotective — she doesn't pass on my messages, she waits on the extension to hear what I'm going to say. Do you think it's fair and what can I do about it? Do you think my girlfriend's being an only child is the problem? By the way, my mother thinks I'm a pretty great guy.

I'm impressed to see you've listed your mom as a character reference — a nice touch. Perhaps you could follow up this avenue by asking for some motherly advice from her. After all, she *is* an expert.

"Only" children are in a peculiar position. By the time their parents are child-rearing experts, their child is about to leave home. With no other kids in the house, they have no one left to practice their new skills on. It sounds like her mom is spying out of fear — the fear of not knowing what's going on between you and her only daughter. Her behavior is less than exemplary, but when you're seventeen and living at home, you aren't in a position of power, so there's not much your girlfriend can do to force a change.

Sometimes the best approach is to give her mother what she wants: information. Here's one trick you can try on the next eavesdropping occasion: make a flattering remark about your girlfriend's mom and see what happens. Sometimes you just have to be strategic.

My fiancée and I are getting married in three months. At least, that's the plan. Unfortunately, my future in-laws hate me. I haven't done anything to warrant their distaste, and I know it's putting a huge strain on my fiancée. Is there a future for me in a family that seems to wish I was posted to another galaxy?

A Don't give up hope. Sometimes families put up a barrier that only the strong can pass. In other words, if they can scare you off easily, too bad for you. Often in these situations, though, once they know you aren't going to disappear, they incorporate you into the system. I say wait them out. If they don't come around later, you can always develop a headache at opportune moments — like just before leaving for Uncle Ernie's retirement dinner. Two adults should be able to make their own future — and their own family.

Q **My girlfriend and I are planning to get married this summer. My problem is that she comes from a big family and has always wanted a huge production with hundreds of people. It really means a lot to her. I, on the other hand, am an only child. I have few relatives, and looked forward to a small ceremony. What do we do?**

A A wedding is the stapling together of two people, both of whom have differing ideas on life and how it should be lived. No doubt this is merely the first of many altercations, arguments, and debates in your joined future. The important thing is to communicate how you feel. Perhaps you can compromise and have a small, intimate ceremony and then a reception that includes the cast of thousands.

I'm not sure who's paying for this production, but the person with the purchasing power usually has more deciding power. Also, you might consider the advantages of just giving in to the idea of a grand extravaganza. Since your family is smaller anyway, you'll have lots of time at the reception to get to know Uncle Vito, Cousin Luis, Auntie Yoko, and all the rest. That way, you'll know which ones you like well enough to invite over for dinner and which to avoid like the plague. And there's another advantage to a big wedding, of course: lots of presents. This comes in handy if you're in need of a new breadmaker, toaster oven, or set of matching towels.

Talk it over with your wife-to-be. If she really has her heart set on the bash to end all bashes, will it really be the end of the world for you? If the score is tied, then the person who feels more strongly should win. In this match, that sounds like her.

My older sister is always telling me what to do. We're both grown up now, but she acts more like a parent than a sibling. Is there anything I can do to get her to realize I'm not twelve years old any more?

Whether you are the youngest, oldest, middle, or only child in your family plays a big role in your perspective of the world, and your place in it. No, it's not like astrology where you can look up a star chart and predict your future, but there is no doubt that life looks different to the first-born daughter than it does to the last. Eldest children get to be instructors, helping to teach the younger kids about growing up. Youngest children have no one to teach, but a lot of instructors to listen to.

As we get older, we try to break free of the kinds of roles we had in our family, even if we don't really realize what those roles actually were, or how we were influenced by them. It sounds to me like you are the youngest child insisting on running her own life, while she is the older sister who still has the habit of trying to run it for you. Now that you're an adult, you want to reposition yourself in the family. Try being unpredictable and doing something that breaks out of the "youngest child" mold. For example, go over to your older sister and adjust her hair, or pull her aside and give her *your* opinion on how to handle Daddy's midlife crisis. I'd bet you'll get a different reaction from Sis this time around.

Q My husband and I have never been self-conscious about walking around the house nude when no one else was about (like after a shower, for example). Now our daughter is two years old and she's really starting to notice things. Should we be covering up so she doesn't end up staring at Daddy's private parts?

A There are two schools of thought on this. One is that once a child is old enough to figure out that there are two sexes, the body parts of both should be covered up. The other is that being comfortable with your body, including your unclothed body, is perfectly natural; therefore, it shouldn't be treated as something embarrassing that needs to be hidden from sight.

Most children develop a natural sense of modesty some time before their teenage years. At that point, they will no longer be comfortable being seen without their clothes, and will probably groan if they see you or your husband without yours. Whether you subscribe to the early modesty theory or not, you should probably be covering up by then.

Q Our little girl is five and loves to get in the bath with my wife and myself. With all the public concern about sexual abuse, I wonder at what age this practice should be stopped.

A You have a bathtub that fits your wife, yourself, and your five-year-old? Sounds more like a lap pool.

Families come in two kinds: those who are comfortable with nudity, and those who are not. Since it appears your family falls into the former category, I wouldn't worry too much about what age is the right time to stop. At some point, your daughter will let you know. She will either tell you outright she wants to bathe alone (small kids don't worry about hurting feelings, they just blurt things out), or she will start covering up hers while pointing at yours and saying, "Gee, Mom and Dad, that's so gross!" At that point, you and your wife can go back to having your baths-for-two, and you'll probably enjoy them more anyway, since your daughter will no longer be there to cramp your style.

As for the public concern over your current family bath, forget about it. You can't live your life in fear of nosy neighbors butting into matters you know are purely innocent. Otherwise, you drive yourself crazy.

After four years of trying to have a baby, my husband and I finally turned to fertility drugs. I did become pregnant, but later had a miscarriage. The baby would soon have been a year old, and I'm feeling really depressed again. Any tips to get me through these hard times?

For most women, a miscarriage is just as bad as losing a baby, and therefore you're facing all the same stages of loss and grief. Don't compound your situation by thinking you don't have the right to feel the pain — you do. If the sadness gets too bad, there are grief counselors who can help. In the meantime, you should lean on your loved ones, take it one day at a time, and remember the old saying that applies perfectly to you at this point: time heals.

I'm married to a wonderful guy and we have a fabulous relationship. My problem is my father-in-law. Every time we go to his house, he stares at my breasts, and I get really uncomfortable.

I haven't talked to my husband about it because I don't want to make things difficult for him, but now I really don't like going to my in-laws' house. What should I do?

A I guess you don't want to wear a loose turtleneck coat in the house all the time? Then my second suggestion would be that next time this happens, look at your father-in-law and announce in a loud voice, "What is it, did I drop fondue on my chest? What are you staring at?" Still, don't be too hard on the guy — after all, he's just enjoying the view. As for your husband, it's probably nothing that needs to be discussed. It will just make him feel uncomfortable, and there's not much he can do anyway.

Q The first orgasm I ever remember was when I was twelve and rolling around on the floor with my younger brother. He's now twenty-one and gay. I worry that I made him gay, and I worry that I abused him while we were playing. I avoid seeing him because the memory makes me uncomfortable. Am I crazy, or what?

A No, you're not crazy, and no, you didn't make him gay. Sexual orientation is firmly implanted long before we play doctor. Children have orgasms — it's simply a physiological fact. In fact, fetuses in the womb have been observed on ultrasound scans with erections. Your brother probably doesn't even remember the incident that haunts you today, and even if he does remember, he also no doubt recalls that you were both children at the time. Your behavior was appropriate to your age. Take this silly little memory, write it down on a piece of paper, and bury it somewhere. That should take care of that. Then phone your brother — he's probably bothered more by your unexplained absence than by anything else.

My daughter is approaching the age when she needs to know about the birds and the bees. There seems to be a big controversy right now over sex education in the schools. Where do you stand on the issue?

The two sides currently seem to be battling over whether kids need more sex education, or less. Back in the 1950s, sex education for girls consisted of your mother telling you that boys have a penis, and you should stay away from it. Boys were heartily clapped on the back at age sixteen by a friendly uncle, handed a condom, and left to sort things out on their own. Usually, the condom was carried around for a couple of years like a badge of courage, then used as a water balloon.

The people who are anti-sex-education believe that if their children have too much information about sex, they'll start having sex. The argument is that if you tell someone about something, they will immediately go out and do it. But parents have been mentioning homework for years, and that hasn't made anyone jump to it. In reality, as often as not, too much information leads to lack of interest in the subject in general.

Where do I stand on sex education? I'm in favor of all education. Children and teens process information much more wisely than their adult supervisors would like to believe. Considering the number-one reason why young teens indulge in sex is curiosity, better to hand out the information so that they don't all have to do their own experiments.

Q At a wedding recently, my mother-in-law made a drunken pass at me, believe it or not. My wife is the jealous type and she'd go nuts if she knew. I don't want to split up our family, but I never want to see my mother-in-law again, either. Can you offer some guidance?

A First of all, never tell your wife. After all, it is her mother, drunk or otherwise. When your mother-in-law is sober, you can privately approach her. Let her know you understand she never would have made a pass at you if she hadn't been drinking. Tell her you've chosen to forget the whole incident, and also let her know that if it ever happens again, you'll probably scream very loudly, and make a spectacle of her. Having said that, never mention the event again, and carry on at family gatherings as if it really never had happened.

Q I've heard stories from my uncle about the "good old days" when my parents were my age, and it sounds to me like they had a lot more fun. I know my mom and dad had lovers before they met each other, but now they're lecturing me about waiting and being careful and taking enough precautions to survive a nuclear war. Is this just the old double standard, or is the sexual revolution really over?

A Let's face it, most parents would prefer that their children never had sex. Okay, maybe once or twice to create grandchildren. Parents have a really hard time recognizing their children as sexual beings, even after they are fully grown adults. Add in the scourge of STDs that can kill, and now *all* parents prefer that their children never have sex.

I once heard it put this way: the sexual revolution is not over — it's just that more of the troops are dying. The urge to merge is no different today than in the 1950s, '60s, or '70s — or the *18*70s, for that matter. The difference is in how people deal with their desires, and how they act on them. The rise of AIDS has led to the quite legitimate fear that sex can be deadly. It's a feeling humankind has had before: in the days before penicillin, when STDs like syphilis were killers, instead of nuisances treatable with antibiotics.

What is different today is the menu of available alternatives. People talk sex over phone lines, and type sex over the Internet, both of which could be called "the new safe sex." Others spend their time playing with the presexual energies and tensions between people, rather than actually having sex itself. More people are hanging out in groups, fascinated with but staying away from sex. And still others, mostly in the younger age groups, rely on their feelings of immortality to protect them from the scourges of the times in which we live. Unfortunately, it is this last group, as always, who will bear the highest casualty rate of this stage of the sexual revolution. Teenagers and people in their early twenties are already contracting STDs at a much higher rate than their elders. They'll be the ones paying the highest prices a decade or more down the road.

My next-door neighbors make a lot of noise having sex, and it's driving me nuts. I'm not a prude, but I have to wear headphones and crank up the stereo in order to get any peace. Then I have to face them in the lobby the next morning and pretend nothing's wrong. How can I ask them to tone it down without embarrassing them and myself?

A Next time you see them in the lobby, say, "I don't know what the walls are made of in this place, but they sure don't block any sound. I don't know what you were watching on TV last night, but it sounded like a big orgy and I could hear every grunt and moan. Maybe you could do me a favor and move your TV set away from that wall?" If that doesn't get results, they clearly don't care whether you sleep or not. Your next call may have to be to the landlord.

Q I live in a college residence with three other women. One of my roommates regularly lets her boyfriend sleep over, and they shower together while the rest of us are trying to sleep (and they do more than wash, and they do it loud enough that the rest of us know it). Should we confront her about it, or just live with it? Is there a way to drop her some subtle hints that we're not happy?

A They're doing the wet and wild loud enough to wake the weary and you want to be subtle? These people wouldn't know subtle if it jumped up and bit their tushes. I think this scenario calls for the blunt approach. Next time they come out of the shower, try hitting him with a bill for laundering his part of the towels and heating his share of the water. Then ask if he'd mind pitching in for some food as well. In other words, start treating him as if he is financially, emotionally, and physically responsible for things going on in the household under whose roof he's spending so much time.

Once your current problem is remedied, you might want to lay down some house rules concerning sex on the premises. For example, no sex when others are home, or an arrangement where some of you go out on alternating nights, in order to leave a window of opportunity and privacy open for the one who stays behind.

Q I just found out one of my best friends is gay. Now I'm uncomfortable when I'm around him, and I feel guilty about feeling uncomfortable. How can I get rid of these feelings?

A What makes you uncomfortable? Your friend is exactly the same person he was the day before you found out he was gay. All that has changed is that you now know something new about the one percent of his life that has to do with sex. And what of that? We all have more in common than we have apart when it comes to sexual orientation. We have the same sorts of feelings, the same hopes and expectations. The only real difference between homosexuals and heterosexuals is to whom they are attracted. That's it. We all pick up our dry cleaning, floss our teeth, and put our pants on one leg at a time.

So why exactly are you uncomfortable? Maybe it's because you've been caught by surprise. If so, it's a natural reaction — the news is new and unexpected. Once it becomes old news, it will have much less impact. Most important, remember this redundant truism: a friend is a friend is a friend.

Q Why does my male friend always manage to turn our conversations into sexual overtures?

A I'm assuming that you are not laughing at any of his feisty remarks — that would probably be seen as encouraging. Some guys think that the best foreplay is Talking About Sex. It goes something like this: once you're yakking about It, then you're thinking about It. Once you're thinking about It, then you're doing It. It's one of the oldest ploys around.

Commonplace or humorous it may be, but that's beside the point. Friends should not smother you with unwanted sexual conversations — it's just plain rude. Sounds to me like your so-called friend is actually lobbying for the position of lover, and has taken an approach you find uncomfortable. You can first try changing the subject whenever he makes his unwanted overtures. If he doesn't understand the gentle hint, hit him with a full-powered, full-volume, verbal description of his lack of manners.

My boyfriend and I broke up about six months ago, and just recently we got back together. The problem is that while we were separated, he dated someone I know quite well. While we were apart, it was no problem, but now that we're back together, there's a tension when the three of us are together, even though we all know no one did anything wrong. How can we get comfortable with one another again?

You may want to break up the communication pattern here, from triangular to straight-line, one on one. You say you "know her well." If that means she's a friend, replace the old history with some new events together. Have lunch, go out, build on the parts of your friendship that don't include your boyfriend. After some time has passed, my guess is that things will become much more comfortable again. Sometimes clichés are valid — in this case, three really *is* a crowd.

I was visiting some friends in Seattle recently and we went to a restaurant downtown. Imagine my shock when I looked up and saw my friend's husband, all lovey-dovey with another

woman. There was no mistaking the fact that this was <u>not</u> just a business lunch, and while I saw him clearly, he never saw me. My problem now is, do I tell my friend, or keep out of it?

A Don't you hate those moments when people take dumb chances and *their* behavior becomes *your* problem? Well, the truth is, it isn't your problem, exactly, unless you let it be. It is not your job to announce his indiscretions. This is a matter between him and his wife, and despite your evaluation of the situation, there could be extenuating circumstances about which you know nothing.

That said, you would not be out of line to confront your friend's husband directly. Feel free to let him know you saw him in Seattle, and that if you spotted him, others could easily have seen him as well. This kind of situation is always a difficult call, but generally I think you should either deal with the person directly, or keep silent.

Q I would really like to tell this certain woman that I'm not interested in her, but I don't know how. To be honest, I've never been in this situation before, and I don't want to hurt her feelings. Should I tell her in person?

A Never date someone because you feel sorry for them — no one needs a pity date. Whether you tell her in person or not depends on the situation. If she's asked you out, make it clear from the beginning that while you like her as a person, a romantic relationship is just not going to happen. You may recognize this as something a woman told you sometime in your own life. You probably didn't like it at first, but later on, you appreciated being told sooner rather than later, and so will she. On the other hand, if she's harassing you or just being really persistent, you may want to go with a more distant rejection.

Whichever way you choose, do not leave a message on her answering machine. That is the kind of thing that third parties inevitably overhear, and embarrassing her in front of her family, friends, or whomever is unfair to both of you.

Q I recently moved to a new city and started a new job. Two weeks later, imagine my shock when I ran into an old ex-boyfriend in the company cafeteria. It's not like he's stalking me or anything — I really believe it's pure coincidence (we broke up six years ago and I haven't seen him since). Anyway, now here we both are, and I think we're both uncomfortable about it. What do I do?

A The first order of business is to decide whether the two of you are going to: (a) pretend you never met; (b) pretend you once met at some function or other but really don't know each other too well; or (c) let the people around you know you once had a relationship, but don't any more. Once you decide which scenario you're going to enact, the rest of the problem will become much easier.

I'd suggest the two of you have coffee somewhere away from the company cafeteria, and come to a decision together. You've both lived a lot of life since you were together. What happens from here on is a new history between you, not the old story revisited. Your new history may include sharing jelly donuts in the cafeteria, or working on a project together, and the fact that you were once a couple is more an interesting coincidence than a major news flash. No one in your new city knows about your old relationship except the two of you, so it will become only as big a deal as you make it.

I'm twenty-four, I'm straight, and I'm constantly being hit on by gay guys. Please don't get me wrong — I'm not homophobic. I'm just getting tired of saying, "Sorry, you're a nice guy, but I'm not gay." Is there anything I can do to avoid this problem?

I'll assume you're not spending a lot of time in gay bars or bookstores, where the clientele could safely infer you might be available. Some people attract lots of attention, others none at all. Apparently, you're really attractive, but you're not unique. In one study, 64 percent of the men surveyed said they had been hit on by a gay man. About 30 percent said it happened a lot. No doubt it happens more frequently in a cosmopolitan city in California than in a small town in Texas, but obviously it's no rare occurrence.

Short of wearing a T-shirt announcing your sexual orientation, I know of no easy way for you to totally avoid the attentions of others. For now, all I can suggest is that you continue to be light-hearted. Don't take it all too seriously while you just say thanks, but no thanks.

I'm in my mid-thirties, all my friends are having kids, and I don't want any. Is there something wrong with me? Am I being selfish?

How can you be selfish? You're going to be the only person in your group with enough time to babysit all their kids. No, I'm not suggesting you have a child in self-defense. What I am suggesting is that since the people around you are going to have them, you'll probably be best off learning how to at least have a relationship with children. There's nothing wrong with not wanting to have a child of your own. Many people prefer pets, or just living solo. Children do not provide a yardstick to measure a person's success as a human being, nor are they an indication of how caring a person you are.

How can I tell if my friend is a lesbian? She's been acting a little strange lately and I'm beginning to question her sexuality.

There's no way to tell a person's sexual orientation just by looking. The simplest way to find out would be to ask her, but first ask yourself a question: does it really matter? If she's your friend, and if you enjoy each other's company, why should you care whether she's sexually attracted to men or women? Gay or straight or somewhere in between, she's still the same person you've always known.

If your anxiety stems from the fear that she will come on to you, then you have two choices. One is to be flattered, and consider it as you would an approach from a guy you aren't interested in that way. Or you can let your friend know that although you accept her own sexuality, she should accept the fact that yours is different. Before you choose, remember this: a lesbian is not necessarily going to lurch onto the first woman she meets, any more than a straight man is likely to dive onto the first woman *he* sees. Don't flatter yourself too much — whether she's gay or not, you may not be your friend's type anyway.

5

Quirks and Curiosities

Just as each of us has unique fingerprints and genetic makeup, so we all have our own unique sexual profiles. One person might consider anything beyond the missionary position to be outrageously kinky. To another, sex is mundane if not performed in the pretzel position in an elevator. What you or I think of another person's leanings is irrelevant — any private sexual behavior that hurts none of the participants is within the realm of one's own private life and should not be held up for applause or condemnation by the rest of the world. Some people squeeze lemon on everything they eat. Others prefer hot sauce. It's all a matter of taste.

Of course, no matter how tame your real sex life is, what goes on in the confines of your cranium can be something entirely different. By definition, fantasies are private, and until recently, few people ever shared their intimate daydreams with one another. Then someone wrote a book on the subject, and before you could say "bestseller," one's fantasy life became suitable material for casual conversation.

I think this is a good thing. As long as people kept their dreams confined to the darkest recesses of their minds, they were left to ponder whether their fantasies were proper. "Is this good, A-class material, or is there something terribly wrong with me?" Once people brought their fantasies into the daylight of ordinary conversation, their questions began being answered, if they'd believe the opinions they received.

People have fantasies about all kinds of things they'd never attempt in real life. Whether your dream involves winning the lottery or making love to an entire football team simultaneously, there's no foul called in fantasy. The difficulty begins when people follow the logic, "I have a fantasy, it is pleasurable, therefore I should act it out." If your dream involves winning a million dollars or the Nobel Prize in physics, there's probably no harm in trying, even if it doesn't work out. If your fantasy involves making love with your best friend and her boyfriend, it's very difficult to brush it off and walk away if the reality turns out to be the disaster the dream never could be.

 What kinds of things drive a guy's imagination crazy?

 Two beautiful, very large-breasted, long-legged, naked women lusting after him. Enough said.

 What drives a woman's imagination crazy?

A guy with slow hands who thinks three hours of foreplay is about right, after he's washed the dishes.

Okay, seriously, then: the truth is that what it takes to turn a woman on may be completely different from what it takes to get a guy going. In general, men are more visual creatures. They may be aroused by lingerie, candlelight, and pictures of gorgeous naked women. On the other hand, women may be more stimulated by the idea that the kids are not going to be interrupting the festivities, or by the feeling that they are truly appreciated. This means that the best way to turn your man on may be climbing into a new red lace teddy before he gets home from work. The best way to turn your woman on may be to clean the other day-to-day business off the plate before she gets home from work. And then, when she does, take the time to let her appreciate the luxury of having nothing mundane to do, before you head for the bedroom.

Why are so many heterosexual men obsessed with the idea of watching two women make love?

Number one on the list is that most men imagine themselves joining the action. In other words, in their own fantasy, they're not just spectators.

Another factor here is that most men probably aren't too sure how a woman actually works. This is likely due to the fact that in the genital department, men's are outies hanging in plain view at all times, while women's are innies, mostly hidden from sight where they can remain mysterious. Because of this, perhaps men think, at some unconscious level, that they'll learn things by watching how two women find pleasure together. Also, whether homosexual or heterosexual, most men would probably agree that from a purely visual standpoint, a woman's body is more aesthetic. In other words, two women making love would be some-how more artistic than two men.

Why are so many men obsessed with the idea of making love with two women?

The idea seems to be if one is good, two is better, and a crowd is even better than that. Of course, he knows he couldn't possibly take care of all this activity simultaneously — that is why for the vast major-ity of men, the ménage à trois remains a fantasy they aren't about to ful-fil. Those who do try this adventure may not find it measures up to their fantasy. As a sexual sage once said: If man were meant to have group sex, he would have more penises.

Before dating my current boyfriend, I had a crush on a guy who has always considered me "just a friend." I never did pursue him, and I'm happy with my boyfriend, but I still fanta-size occasionally about him. I don't know what to do about this problem.

People often fantasize, especially about people who are unat-tainable. This other guy only likes you as a friend, so he's safe — there's no way this relationship-of-the-mind is going to take any turns that will tie your life in knots. It's really no different than married guys fantasizing about supermodels and movie stars: dream on. In other words, you real-ly don't have a problem, as long as your fantasy isn't disturbing you.

Rodney Dangerfield once joked about a night when he and his wife couldn't find the mood, so he turned to her and asked, "What's the matter? Couldn't you think of anyone else either?"

What does it mean when your boyfriend is dreaming about hot times with his old flame? What do you think I should do about it?

I'd be less concerned about the dream than about the fact that he's telling you about it. We have little control over the content of our sleeping movies of the mind. Another guy might simply enjoy the dream and forget about it, rather than passing along a recitation to his current girlfriend. If he keeps giving you a replay each morning, maybe there's something else he's trying to tell you. Ask him.

I've been having this recurring erotic dream that's driving me nuts. After countless sleepless nights, now I can't help thinking about it during the day as well, and it's affecting my job and home life. I've tried humming obnoxious TV theme songs and counting the spots on the acoustic tile above my head, but nothing works. Is there anything that can help me?

The only destructive fantasies I can think of are those that you feel you can't control. Any time that a dream is uncomfortable, disturbs you, and is taking over your waking life, then I think you should be looking for professional help. There are times when your mental equilibrium can be thrown off by psychological causes or stress, but the root of your problem may be physical as well — perhaps a metabolic or hormonal imbalance. Just as some people suffer from an iron deficiency or the lack of a certain vitamin, others have a lack of some chemical essential to keep the head in tune.

Unfortunately, many people are reluctant to seek help for things that can't be pinned down to a cut or a scrape or a broken bone. But a problem that seems to involve your mind is no different from one involving your forearm. Both are parts of your body, and both have professionals trained to help you with them. When your car breaks down, maybe you try to fix it yourself, but if you can't, you see your mechanic. Treat yourself at least as well as you treat your Jeep — go see an expert.

I've been having cybersex with a flirtatious girl I met on the Internet a few weeks ago. When I told my wife about it, she hit the roof and demanded I stop. I've met a lot of new friends on the chatlines, and I don't want to give it up. It's only a computer I'm talking to, isn't it? So how can I be cheating on my wife by talking to a computer?

There are two kinds of cybersex, and in my mind they have different implications. If you're involved in a Multi-User Dimension, or MUD, you're creating a character and letting him act out an ever-changing scenario, one that includes all the other MUDders out there, along with their own characters. This category of cybersex is no more a case of cheating than writing a steamy novel would be, or playing a board game. A novelist is not his characters, and you're not the fantasy character you invent in cyberspace. On the other hand, if you and your cyber-mate are communing over the Internet Relay Chat lines (IRC), then what you are having is the computerized version of phone sex.

The whole issue of cybersex is a product of the wildly changing times in which we live, and the definitions are fuzzier than scuzzy-logic. Your wife's real problem may be the amount of time you're spending on-line with your cybermate, as opposed to off-line with her. She might be equally upset if you were spending all your time watching raunchy movies, instead of being intimate with her. It's all a question of looking, rather than touching. I'd say that if your hands are on the keys while you create your Internet scenario, you're a cyber-writer. If one or both hands are in your lap, you're having e-sex.

I'm a woman who's always had bisexual fantasies, and the other night, while drinking with my girlfriend, we ended up having sex. The next morning, she seemed embarrassed by the whole event, and pretty much refuses to talk about it. What should I do?

Consider yourself educated in two of the reasons why one-night stands don't generally work out very well. First, you've learned that drinking and sexual regrets often go hand in hand. Second, you've discovered that when people have sex without much forethought, there's less chance the relationship will end up being anything more than a one-nighter. It seems obvious your friend is not available for any further relationship — she's embarrassed and doesn't want to discuss it. The best thing you can do right now is consider that if the same events had taken place with a guy, you would probably shrug it off and go on with your life. The fact that it was a woman, rather than a man, really doesn't change the circumstances. You have to respect the fact that she doesn't want to go any further, and that you are going to be left on your own to process this event. Treat it as a sexual experience that didn't work out, because that's what it is.

Q I have a girlfriend I've been seeing for four years, and there's a couple in the picture who are our good friends. To make a long story shorter, we're thinking about having sex with each other's partner. We've all talked about it, we're all consenting adults. My question is, what kind of problems might we encounter afterward, if we go ahead with the temporary trade?

A For those who have played the friendly game of musical beds, or indulged in group sex, the most common complaint is that quite often, the two people who most enjoyed the party did not arrive at it together. This of course leaves the rest of the group picking up the pieces of their relationships, and going home alone. Unless you can guarantee that emotions won't get mixed up with genitals — and you can't — then you have to be prepared for the fact that the configuration of partners may look a lot different coming out than it did going in. If you feel this very real risk is too great, you'd probably be best off keeping partner-trading as a fantasy — dreaming about tasting a different taco won't cost you the whole enchilada.

Q I'm thirty pounds overweight but working on it. Now my husband is getting jealous, and says he'll have to keep a closer eye on me once I'm thin. How can I get him to cool it?

A People don't lose weight for other people, they do it for themselves. If your husband wants to keep you less attractive to others, then perhaps he'd also like you to wear a Richard Nixon Halloween mask whenever you go to the supermarket. Is his message that he wants to be the only person who finds you captivating? Or is it that you can't be trusted, and once you're skinny, your personality will change and you'll be off picking up stray men? Unfortunately, cooling his jealousy may be harder than losing the weight. I think the issues you need to address with him center on trust and insecurity, not your dress size.

My husband and I enjoy experimenting sexually, but it takes such a long time to receive things by mail order. Personally I am terrified to walk into the sex shops in my city. Can you give me some alternatives where I'll be comfortable?

First of all, be proud of your sexual experimentation. Many people decide their marriage is boring but continue in the navel-to-navel position throughout their life. As for adult stores, while there were once hundreds across the continent, many have gone out of business because of competition from loverware parties (just like Tupperware and lingerie parties). All the things that wiggle and jump and sing and hum can now be brought to your own home, to be examined in the comfort of your living room, in the company of close friends. The owners of sex shops still in business tell me that most of their clientele are respectable couples coming in on their lunch hours, so don't be afraid to walk in. As a third option, remember that many of the turbocharged gizmos that used to be the exclusive domain of the sex shop are now found on the shelves of your average department store. True, they may say they're for massaging the feet or neck, but they sure look just like those made for stimulating your other body parts. They work the same, too.

Whenever I have sex, I end up thinking about my roommate. I'm very attracted to him, but I don't know how to approach him. Any ideas?

A It's seldom a good idea to hit on your roommate. Good roommates are incredibly hard to come by, whereas sexual partners litter the landscape. Someone who shares your taste in TV shows, who folds and stacks the laundry, and who doesn't drink milk from the container — that's a person who is truly awe-inspiring. If you have one of those great relationships where you and your cohabitant have little dissension and are happily living under the same roof, under no circumstances should you mess with it. One of the more likely outcomes of trying is that you end up looking for a new address.

Also, just because you dream about your roomie doesn't mean you should hit on him. It's often better to keep a fantasy a fantasy, rather than trying to turn it into a reality that won't live up to the expectations you've built around it. Lots of people feel that every time you have a sexual thought about another human being, you should act on it. It's true that some fantasies turn out to be fantastic in real life, but often, people find them a great disappointment.

Q **I'm a police officer, and my wife is excited by having sex in risky, public situations while I'm still in uniform. I confess some of this turns me on, but I don't want to get caught making love with my wife in a squad car, and end my career in the process. What should I do?**

A You probably want to start by sitting your wife down at home and finding out what kind of stresses she is under that would lead her to pressure you into such situations. Remind her that while having sex in your cruiser at high noon in the mall parking lot may give her a thrill, she won't be so excited by the prospect of your trying to make mortgage payments and pay grocery bills when you're unemployed. Perhaps she'd be happy if you brought your uniform home and pretended to be on duty while you have sex on the kitchen table or the rec room floor. ("Gee, ma'am, is this where you spotted the prowler?" I don't know — write a script!)

Most people don't expect to be able to have sex on company time, regardless of their occupation. Being a police officer means being responsible for the public trust. Remind your wife it's not professional to be caught with your pants down when the burglar alarm goes off.

My husband of ten years recently told me he wants to experiment with men. He says he doesn't think he's gay, but he's always been curious about that side of sex, and he wants to try it out before he's too old. He also says he still loves me and wants to stay married, and it wouldn't exactly be cheating because it wouldn't be another woman. I was so stunned when he told me this, I didn't know what to say. Can you help me find an answer for him?

No, but I can help you find an answer for yourself. It probably makes no difference to you whether his choice of bed partner is male, female, animal, vegetable, or mineral: the important issue here is that it's not you. Your husband obviously has a real talent for rationalizing what he wants to do, and what he wants to do is have a sexual relationship outside the one he has with you. If that is not part of your current agreement, it is unfair bargaining for him to try to justify it.

He says he's not gay, just curious. Well, most people are curious about many things, but that doesn't mean they try them all out. A person may read a book, watch a movie, or ask questions of a gay friend, but to actually fling oneself onto someone of the same sex out of "curiosity"? Seems to me he's not telling you everything. A good percentage of gay men are married to women and have families. Some may be using their families as a cover. Others really do care about their wives and children, even though their sexual orientation is still toward other men.

It seems to me your husband really isn't talking about "curiosity" here. He's talking about attraction. If you talk with him about this and he still insists it's just curiosity about something he's never done, perhaps you could suggest some other activities he's never tried instead, like bungee jumping or rock climbing.

I have discovered that my current girlfriend's favorite things include being tied up, tied down, handcuffed, slapped around, and spanked, just to name a few. I can get into the first level of this sort of thing if it will please her, but she keeps pushing me to actually hurt her physically. That kind of activity is just not my style, to put it mildly. Is there something we can do that will make her happy without forcing me into situations that run so far away from my personal beliefs?

It sounds to me like you'd be happy tying your girlfriend up with loosely knotted lace ribbons that would come undone if she tugged gently on them. She, on the other hand, would prefer to be chained to the wall with padlocks while you wield a bullwhip. I'd say your girlfriend has gotten her arousal system tied into a lot of areas that you don't find stimulating, and I don't know how you can possibly reconcile your desires when they are so far apart.

Social scientists are unsure why different people are turned on by such widely different stimuli. Even so, it is unlikely that she will mute the intensity of her own wants enough to come down to a region in which you feel comfortable, unless she herself is troubled by her desires. People who try to put themselves in painful, difficult, or embarrassing situations often have a history of having these kinds of scenarios forced upon them earlier in life. If your girlfriend fits this picture, you can strongly encourage her to get into counseling to deal with her past hurt, so that she will no longer feel driven to create hurt for herself in the present. Unfortunately, I can't advise you to wait for her even if she does agree to counseling. It rarely turns out that both people end up turned on by the same things, even after putting the past in its place and moving on.

Ⓠ I'm a grown man who likes to wear diapers and be treated like a baby. I have my own pacifiers and rattles and all the necessary accoutrements, but I'm also married and my wife knows nothing of any of this. I've always had to go elsewhere to have these desires fulfilled, but I don't have sex with anyone else, so I don't think I've been a cheating husband. Is there anything wrong with what I'm doing?

Ⓐ "Wrong" is probably the wrong word. The important thing to consider here is how much of your life is taken up sneaking around, pretending to be off at business meetings while you're really shaking your rattle and throwing a tantrum.

There is no doubt that if your wife stumbles across your collection of oversize diapers and baby toys, she's going to be asking herself two serious questions: Is there something going on you're not telling her? Or is she the last one to find out she's pregnant? Take a guess which alternative is more likely.

The fact that you're not having sex outside your marriage means you can honestly say you're not cheating, but you can hardly say you're being totally honest, either. The other problem here is that there is a hugely important part of your life that you are not sharing with your wife, one that you take elsewhere in secret and pay others to share instead.

The fact that you've asked whether this situation is right or wrong tells me that you are not completely at ease with what you're doing, so you may have answered your own question with the question itself. I don't know if your wife would be interested in indulging your infantilism even if you did tell her about it, but perhaps your first step would be to examine the entire issue with a counselor. It wouldn't surprise me if there was some traumatic event in your early childhood that has led to your love of diapers and baby toys. It may just be your way of getting the nurture you missed at an earlier age. Getting an insight into the root of your preoccupation may not change it, but it may leave you with the kind of understanding that will allow you to accept that part of yourself, rather than sneaking around and trying to hide it.

As one who happens to find ladies' feet beautiful, I'm wondering what your opinion is on the subject. Is this common, or a rare type of fetish?

As far as fetishes (or paraphilias) go, it's fairly common. For some devotees, the turn-on is the foot itself. For others, it's the shoe, and for still others, it's the smell of the foot or the shoe. I'd guess you'd find foot fetishists working in shoe stores (no, not *all* shoe salespeople!), and it's safe to bet they're the kind of people who'd like giving long, slow foot massages. Perhaps that's why a lot of partners find it's one fetish that's not too hard to take.

My boyfriend and I like to do stuff to spice up our sex life and people think we're crazy. Like for instance, we like having sex in elevators. I think it's just good-natured fun. What do you think?

A I think it's fine. You're both healthy, happy individuals who like having sex in out-of-the-way places. Why not an elevator? It's private, you're not hurting anybody — from that point of view, it's perfectly acceptable.

One thing you should consider, however, is the crowd of people on the ground floor. They're silently cursing as they wait for the elevator that seems to be stuck on the eighth floor, but is actually not moving because you're holding the door open with your bare butt. The crowd's perception might be that you are being greedy, self-centered, and unfeeling, for making them wait on your pleasure. In other words, just make sure the places you pick for your pleasure don't get in the way of anyone else's good time.

Q My girlfriend keeps needling me to have sex in a public place. She's hinted about the glass elevator in a downtown office tower and the botanical gardens dome on the other side of town. I'll admit the idea is kind of exciting, but I'm apprehensive. Is this a good idea?

A It's a good idea if you've ever had a longing for public embarrassment or worse. Making love in public where others can see you is a criminal offense in many places. If you want to keep your freedom, and your eligibility to be bonded, I'd suggest you consider adventures in less-populated public places. If the elevator idea is a must, try an elevator *without* glass sides, and preferably in a building that's been closed for the night (as long as you're not trespassing, that is). Bear in mind that, Hollywood movies notwithstanding, you cannot stop most elevators between floors without setting off the alarm, unless you have the key. Other less-risky public places include parked cars, the bed of a pickup parked on a seldom-used back road, or in the high grass of your favorite field — as long as it's not the point of convergence of three hiking trails.

A man goes into a public bathroom, does his business, and gets out, with hardly a glance at the guy standing next to him. A woman goes into a public bathroom, makes six new friends, exchanges recipes, and hangs out for an hour. I've always wondered, why the differences?

In this case, gender differences may be sparked by genital differences. Yours hang out for all to see. Hers are tucked away, for the most part invisible, even when she's as naked as the day she was born.

When you stand at the urinal, you may feel exposed and vulnerable, so the last thing you want to do is acknowledge the guy standing next to you. He, too, has his equipment dangling out in the cool breezes, so he's perfectly happy to go along. As a result, men mostly stare at the tile in front of their noses, and pretend they're alone, even when guys are lined up three deep to take their turn.

On the other side of the wall are the women, who do all their bathroom business behind the closed doors of a cubicle. Maneuvering in this small space can stretch a quick visit into a major dance routine — imagine trying to remove pantyhose, juggle a purse, and avoid actually sitting on the seat. When the whole ordeal is over, the payoff is that when women make it to the sinks, they can then spend lots of leisurely time putting on their lipstick, and chatting about the movie, the play, or, more likely, you. Yes, women do talk about men in the bathroom.

Is it true that exhibitionists are attracted to nudist camps?

A nudist camp has about as much appeal to an exhibitionist as a oil spill does to an environmentalist. People accustomed to nudity are hardly going to be shocked by the sight of another naked body. Exhibitionists get their kicks from a stunned, gasping reaction to their display, not a simple "Hi there, new to the club?"

I know it's an old cliché, but I'd really like to have sex in a car. My girlfriend is game, but we've tried three times already and we can't get comfortable. Are we doing something wrong?

No, you're not. Cars have shrunk, while the size of humans has remained the same, which means there's less room for activities other than driving from point A to point B. Adding to the problem is the expanded popularity of the center console, that hump between the bucket seats that's made for your mobile CD collection and/or cellular phone. All of these can make lovemaking less than lovely.

Since the days of Oldsmobile's Delta 88, once known as the "living room on wheels," there has been a shortage of sex-friendly vehicles. You could get yourself a used car, say, one built in Detroit in the early 1960s. You could buy a stretch limo. Or you could dress up your bedroom with hubcaps and a fuzzy car blanket, paste some glow-in-the-dark stars to the ceiling, and pretend you're at the drive-in.

Q I've always wanted to make love with my boyfriend in a swimming pool, but I heard that you can get locked together by water pressure or muscle cramps or something. I even heard about a couple that had to be taken to hospital to get separated. Is this true?

A Not unless you're both scuba-diving at the time and try to ascend to the surface while still attached at the hips (and it probably wouldn't even happen then). The average swimming pool is only three or four feet deep in the shallow end, and you wouldn't be able to generate enough difference in water pressure to create any hydraulic lock between you. As for muscular locking, there are some species that have genital equipment that balloons up during sex. The male is clamped tight and is not allowed to disengage until the act is over. Needless to say, humans don't have this vise-like equipment.

There are, however, other reasons why making love in the pool may be a bad idea. First, the chlorine in the water is not condom-friendly. Second, trying to keep one's head above water in the throes of passion is not much of a turn-on for most people. Third, the water will wash away your natural lubrication, making sex more difficult and less comfortable. This is another case where the movies lie to us, by making sex in the pool look easier and more fun than you may actually find it to be.

Q After six years of marriage, my wife and I drifted apart and eventually divorced. One of the reasons we stayed together as long as we did was that the sex was fantastic. We're still friendly and we're both still single, and occasionally we end up sleeping together. A friend of mine thinks we're nuts. Do you think what we're doing is wrong?

Basically, you and your ex-wife are two single people having sex together. If that sits well with you both, you're not doing anything wrong. The fact that you were once married does not make it more okay or less okay to sleep together now. However, if the relationship is based on nothing more than sex (great as it may be), you might want to consider whether you are shortchanging yourselves. As long as you're doing this dance, you're not really able to get involved with someone else — someone with whom you might also share intellectual and emotional attachments. Right now, a part of you is unavailable for that possible new partner. You risk getting stuck where you are out of convenience.

It takes so much energy to have sex. Is there any danger of that energy loss leading to other problems with your general health?

It takes a fair amount of energy to brush your teeth or do the grocery shopping, too. Are you going to let your teeth rot or stop eating to save energy? We're talking about 150 calories here, more or less — it's not like sex will make you fade away from overexertion. Besides, as any fit person can tell you, exercise gives you more energy, not less. Athletes don't become less tired when they stop competing, and exercise is one of the best remedies for fatigue.

For you trivia buffs, a couple generates about three kilowatts of energy in the ten minutes (on average) that they're involved in sexual intercourse. That's enough energy to light thirty table lamps. If the lifetime sexual energy of the world's population were accumulated, it would equal the release of energy from the explosion of a 1.5-megaton nuclear bomb. There's a lot of energy in sex, but it's the good kind, and it's easily replenishable. Sex is a renewable resource.

Does intercourse really affect the performance of athletes in full-time or part-time training (i.e., "sap their energies")?

Not unless the sport they're training for is what my mother used to call "chesterfield rugby." Although there are teams around the world that do not allow their players to have intercourse with their wives or girlfriends long before the game is played, the idea of sex "sapping your energy" is mere superstition. When it comes to a connection between sex the night before and athletic performance the day after, the only important factor is whether the athlete gets any sleep between the two.

Is sexual intercourse a good way to lose weight?

Unfortunately not. You expend about seven calories per minute in an average lovemaking session. This means a session on the stationary bicycle or rowing machine will go a lot further toward losing the pounds, even if machines in a gym are not exactly as much fun as sex. Of course, if intercourse is your only exercise, it's better than nothing, as long as your idea of foreplay does not include a thousand calories' worth of oysters, Brie, and white wine.

A friend of mine just had her nipples pierced and no matter how open-minded I try to be, it just grosses me out completely. I just don't get it. Why do people pierce their intimate body parts?

Some people may think intimate body piercing is sexual, but I suspect it has more to do with the S&M side of the sexual frontier than the mainstream. Proponents of piercing will tell you that putting holes in your nipples or genitals is sexually arousing. But I can't help thinking these are the people who didn't get enough attention from their second-grade teacher, Miss Pinsky, so they just kept upping the ante until they were noticed. I find this personal belief to be particularly reinforced when I see people with pierced tongues and nipples, walking around with their shirts off and their mouths open.

I also think body piercing in general is a passing fad (who knows, it may be gone by the time you read this sentence). So, if you're looking for a sure thing in a profession, I suggest you seriously consider any occupation whose job description could be summed up as "Body Hole Repairer."

The ABCs
of STDs

For every up, there is unfortunately a down, so it's no surprise that something as much fun as sex would have its own major downers. Warts, bumps, lumps, runny things, and things that glow in the dark (okay, just kidding on the last one) — these are the unpleasant and sometimes deadly side effects that happen when one does not treat sexual behavior with the proper respect. Your genitals are not just the parts of your body that often feel best to you. They are also the warm, moist places that are most attractive to a wide variety of viruses, bacteria, and other microbes, none of which you would willingly invite over for a long-term stay. It's like those places some people consider jungle paradises: there's a lot of spectacular scenery and flora, but also a huge variety of bugs and microbes. We have to share our paradise.

As long as there has been sex, there have probably been sexually transmitted diseases, though different bugs take the spotlight in different eras. Back in the days of World War II, it was syphilis and gonorrhea. Today, it's warts in your privates, genital herpes, and, tragically, AIDS. Even the jargon has changed over the decades. What once was known as VD (venereal disease) is now called STDs (sexually transmitted diseases). What has remained the same all these years is the challenge: how to keep safe, and still have as much fun as possible.

I'm a single woman in my mid-twenties, and I love sex. I have a few different guys I sleep with on a fairly regular basis (safe sex, and one at a time), and I like the variety. I don't think I'm a nymphomaniac or anything, but I can't see settling down with just one man anytime soon. Is there anything wrong with me?

Not yet, but there may be something very wrong with you sometime in the near future. To paraphrase a classic AIDS-prevention slogan, when you sleep with someone, you're also sleeping with everyone they've ever had sex with. The laws of probability dictate that the more sex partners you have, the greater the chance you'll contract something that will be unpleasant, and possibly deadly. You are having what you consider safe sex, but the rest of the world merely considers it safer sex — there is no such thing as completely safe sex. It really doesn't matter whether you have sex with these men one at a time or all at once — the fact is that bacteria and viruses like to hang out on sexual equipment. Getting the variety you like in men means getting acquainted with a much larger variety of microbes.

None of this means you have to immediately settle down with one man. It does mean you should consider whether your present and future health is something that concerns you. The greater the number of partners, the greater the chance you won't have a future to worry about. If you're going to continue having multiple partners, be sure to use protection at all times — in combination if possible, such as condoms combined with a spermicide. If you're having second thoughts about continuing on your present course, remember that you can still have as much sex as you like — sex-for-one is still sex.

How do you tell someone that is dirty and has crabs to get treatment?

"Hey, George! Go to the doctor!" Listen, that's partly what friends are for: to tell their friends the truth, even when it's unpleasant or embarrassing. Just be sure you don't deliver the message naked, in close proximity to your infested friend — pubic lice can jump.

I always thought it was just some silly story our folks told us to scare us, but a friend of mine insists it's actually true — can you really get crabs off a toilet seat?

They jump, so why not? Let's face it, not everything our mothers told us was a myth or misconception. There are many things you can't get from a toilet seat (HIV, syphilis, gonorrhea, chlamydia, to name four), but that doesn't mean you can't get *anything* from a toilet seat. Herpes, crabs, venereal warts — these are possibilities, assuming that you run in and jump on the seat immediately after it's been vacated by an infected person. The key concept here is that few microbes will live for very long on a dry hunk of plastic or porcelain — they just aren't great environments for most germs.

Some public areas do provide relatively friendly spots for micro-organisms, however. If you're going to visit something like a sauna or tanning parlor, you'd probably be best off bringing your own towel for sitting or lying on. Finally, here's the number-one rule for avoiding the non-sexual transmission of sexually transmitted diseases: never, *ever* wear someone else's underwear.

I've been treated once already for genital warts on my penis, and the doctor says I have to go back again. How long does it take to get rid of them?

Unfortunately, sometimes genital warts come back, sometimes they don't, and sometimes it takes more than one treatment to get rid of the first batch you have. How long the treatment will take is best answered by your doctor, as with any sexually transmitted disease. Most of the time, the treatment for men involves painting a compound on the penis to remove them, but this also depends on how long you've had them before treatment begins. In extreme cases, surgery may be required, simply because there are too many to remove otherwise. It's important to make sure you get rid of them all, because not only can you pass them on to your partner, you can also reinfect yourself.

Genital warts are the number-one STD for people under age twenty-five. One study found 70 percent of the people examined carrying them. Also, some kinds have been associated with cervical cancer in women, so they can be more than uncomfortable — they can have deadly complications. Don't wait: if you think you may have genital warts, get to a doctor and find out.

What's the best way to tell if your partner has chlamydia? I hear it's the silent STD.

Yes, it's called the silent STD, because most men and many women have no symptoms at all. That means that even though chlamydia can be easily cured by antibiotics, it becomes serious because so many women don't realize they have it until it has already progressed into pelvic inflammatory disease (PID). Once the disease reaches this stage, it can also produce scarring and infertility. If an infected woman can still have children, she runs the risk of passing the disease to her baby at birth.

Chlamydia is unfortunately fairly easy to contract. The bacteria can find their new home in your body any time two sets of genitals collide, even if no actual intercourse takes place. There's also the danger of moving the bacteria to different parts of your own body — for example, by touching your infected genitals, then rubbing an itchy eye. You can have chlamydia for years if it's not treated, but there is some good news: once diagnosed and treated, it's out of your life.

What's the difference between AIDS and HIV?

At its simplest, the Human Immunodeficiency Virus is the cause, Acquired Immune Deficiency Syndrome is the result, and unfortunately, there is no cure. AIDS is labeled a "syndrome" rather than a "disease," because it is actually a set of complications that set in after HIV has compromised the immune system. This is why you hear of AIDS patients suffering from "rare" diseases like Karposi's Sarcoma. These diseases are rare, but only as long as you have a healthy immune system. This is also why after contracting HIV, it can take up to a decade or more for people to develop AIDS symptoms.

So a person doesn't actually have AIDS until the symptoms appear?

Once the virus is detected, a person is said to be HIV-positive. Generally, you are classed as actually having AIDS either when your T-cell count reaches a certain level, or when the opportunistic infections begin to show up. This long delay between infection and symptoms is also why a blood test is the only sure way of telling whether you've caught the virus. The test does not actually look for HIV itself; rather, it looks for the antibodies your body produces in response to the presence of the virus. This is where the term "HIV-positive" comes from: it means the test has shown a positive result for antibodies to HIV in the blood.

It's important to note that it takes four to six months for your body to produce enough antibodies to be detected in the test. Therefore, your test results are a snapshot of what happened to your body four to six months ago, *not* when the test was taken. This means that you can test negative even though you *are* actually infected, if the infection occurred within the last few months. The only way to be certain you and your partner are both HIV-negative is to take two tests, six months apart, and be absolutely sure you are both celibate or monogamous in between.

As if all of this weren't enough, researchers now believe that HIV is most contagious in the time period immediately after infection. In other words, you can most easily transmit the virus to someone else *before* you even know you have it yourself.

How does the virus get from one person to another?

A HIV is transmitted through body fluids like blood and semen, which is why anal sex is such a high-risk activity. The tissue in that part of your body is not made to stretch the same way a vagina is, so anal intercourse often results in tissue tears. This allows the semen of one person to contact the blood of another. If there is any HIV present, it has an easy path to follow. For much the same reason, intravenous drug use is also a high-risk activity, albeit a non-sexual one. If a needle is shared by two people and there is virus present, then HIV can literally be injected into a new host. If you needed one more reason why drug abuse is a bad idea, there you go.

Q **If I have a cold or flu, could I cause harm to someone who is HIV-positive by being around them?**

A Unfortunately, the answer is yes. A person who is HIV-positive may already have a compromised immune system. And, of course, once it becomes AIDS, it's definitely compromised. This means your friend could easily be far more susceptible to the virus behind your cold or flu, as well as to any bacterial or fungal invaders you may be transporting.

If you're not feeling well, it's not a good time to visit. Phone instead, or drop them a card — there are many ways to let someone know they're in your thoughts, without arriving on their doorstep carrying unwanted microbial company. These same rules also apply to cancer patients, or anyone with other immune system problems.

Can you get AIDS from swallowing semen?

Possibly, if there's a cut in your mouth. The possibility is small, but you should still know your partner's history well before engaging in or performing such intimate acts. Interestingly, saliva seems to have a couple of ingredients that kill HIV, which is why doctors tell you it probably can't be transmitted through kissing. Stomach acid is also probably HIV-unfriendly, but remember that the operative word in both cases is "probably," not "definitely." You still have to ask yourself how much risk is acceptable to you.

What the heck is a dental dam, and what does it have to do with sex anyway?

A dental dam is a usually gray, generally rectangular piece of latex that your dentist attaches to your mouth with a series of wires and gizmos, allowing only the tooth he wants to work on to protrude through. This helps keep the miscellaneous bacteria in your mouth from getting to the tooth your dentist is repairing. The reason it has anything to do with sex is that it is made of latex, and can thus be used as an effective barrier to disease transmission through oral sex.

Most people are not comfortable asking their dentist for a supply, or trying to explain their request to a dental supply house, so they create their own. All you have to do is cut and flatten some condoms and you'll have your own version of the dental dam. Whether you buy or make your own, though, always remember that the dental dam goes on the *genitals*, not the mouth, when it is used sexually. You place it like a dinner napkin on the privates of your female partner (if your partner is a male, have him wear an intact condom) and proceed with oral sex.

A friend of mine went to the doctor recently and was told he has syphilis. What's the deal? I thought syphilis and gonorrhea were extinct diseases.

Don't you wish. The reality is that those two best-known STDs of the previous generation appear to be making a comeback, and antibiotic-resistant strains have been reported as well.

Gonorrhea is what was commonly known as "the clap," and you can have it without any symptoms at all. Men who are infected tend to get a yellow discharge from their penis, and pain when they urinate. Women, on the other hand, often don't notice anything unusual. Most cases of gonorrhea are easily treated with antibiotics, but if left untreated, it can lead to pelvic inflammatory disease and infertility in women, and possibly blindness.

Syphilis is also known to cause blindness if left untreated, as well as sterility, insanity, and/or death. Like gonorrhea, it may give few warning signs. Men will get chancre sores in the first stage of the infection, but then the symptoms usually disappear until the secondary and tertiary infections occur, often with great time lags between. Women often have no symptoms at all. Also like gonorrhea, syphilis is still easily curable with antibiotics, though resistant strains have been reported in some parts of the world.

The bottom line is the same for both: if you notice pain when you urinate, or an odd sore on your genitals, or any unusual discharge, go to your doctor. The sooner you get treatment for any infection, sexually transmitted or not, the better off you'll be.

The other day I got my first cold sore, on my upper lip. Someone told me you can get the STD-type herpes there as well as on your genitals. Is he right? And if so, how can I tell which one I have?

The Herpes simplex virus comes in two flavors, type one and type two. Both cause much the same symptoms, and the difference is primarily one of severity. Herpes One produces what have always been known as "cold sores," red sores that erupt on the skin after some kind of stress, like too much sunlight or a cold (hence the name).

Once you catch it, the virus lives deep in the core of your nerve cells, where it can remain dormant for a long time. At some point, for unknown reasons, it then reactivates and skitters up the nerve fiber until it reaches the skin. That's when it erupts, and when it can be passed around — from one person to another, or from one part of your own body to another (you touch the sore, you touch some other part of your body, and you "auto-infect," to use the jargon).

The Herpes One virus can infect your genitals during oral sex or even masturbation, which would mean you'd then have cold sores on your penis or vagina. Likewise, genital herpes (Herpes Two) can travel from the genitals to the mouth or face in much the same way. Any contact of virus with one of your mucous membranes is all it takes (lips, mouth, vagina, penis), or on a cut on any other piece of your skin. So yes, you can have either type of herpes in either part of your body, or both. As for telling the difference, Herpes Two outbreaks tend to be more painful, but not always.

Unfortunately, there is no cure for a herpes infection, and you'll likely have outbreaks for life, though a small minority have one episode and then never seem to get the blisters again. There are, however, medications available which lessen the severity of the sores, and help get rid of them faster. There are also new treatments being developed regularly.

For the latest on those, call your doctor, local teaching hospital, or university medical center.

I discovered last year that I have genital herpes, and now it seems like I'll be alone forever. Every time I start getting close to someone and it looks like we might have sex, I shy away because I don't want to give them the disease, and I'm too embarrassed to tell them why I can't sleep with them. Is there anything I can do to find someone who'll share my infected life?

First, good for you for being responsible enough to take care not to spread your unwelcome bodily guests to other people. Second, take heart, because you're not alone out there. A study in 1995 concluded that tens of millions of people are infected with one or more of the herpes viruses in the U.S. alone. Whether it's Herpes One or Two really doesn't matter, since the symptoms are much the same (see above). This means that there's a good chance you'll fall for someone who already shares your problem, and will understand what you're going through. It also means you'll have to get over your reticence about telling prospective partners about your problem in the first place.

Of course, even with someone else who's infected, you still want to be careful not to have intimate contact during an outbreak. Even if you both already have the virus, you don't want to spread it around to uninfected parts of your bodies. Incidentally, I'm not saying you should *only* date women who already have herpes. The precautions you take to avoid spreading the virus around your own body are the same ones you take to prevent it from spreading to someone else. If your choice is to date only people who share your predicament, there are groups in many North American cities (and probably around the world) that are set up to help you find each other. Check them out.

Q A friend of mine was diagnosed with cervical cancer recently, and it scared me half to death because she's younger than me! I've also been told that the younger you become sexually active, the greater your risk of developing cancer of the cervix. Is that true, and if so, why?

A It is true, and the reason is simple: the more organisms you allow to enter your body, the greater your chance of contracting any kind of disease, including those that are sexually transmitted.

The most common sexually transmitted infection among people between eighteen and twenty-five years old is human papilloma virus. Cervical cancer is often caused by one of the twenty different HPVs, which are also responsible for genital warts. And while it may not all be attributable to HPV, the risk factors for cancer of the cervix include the age at which intercourse begins (younger is riskier), the number of partners you've had in your sexual life (more is riskier), and whether your sexual activities are protected or unprotected (you guessed it — unprotected is riskier).

Q I've recently read that you can get hepatitis through sexual intercourse, but I've also heard there is more than one kind of hepatitis. Is that right? And if so, which ones do I have to worry about?

A Hepatitis comes by the letters, not the numbers. Specifically, there are three types currently known, called A, B, and C. As you might guess, Hepatitis A is the original of the three, and the one that is *not* transmitted sexually. Both the B and C strains of the disease can be transmitted through intercourse or intravenous drug use, and unfortunately, neither is as easy to cure as the A strain. In fact, as this book goes to print, Hepatitis C is incurable, and the only treatment for B is a liver transplant.

The first symptoms of hepatitis tend to be nausea, headaches, and abdominal pain, followed later by swollen lymph glands, jaundice, and fatigue. The one bit of good news here is that there is now a vaccine against the B strain, so as long as you don't already have it, there is potent protection available. Unfortunately, the vaccine will not protect you from Hepatitis A or C. Your best protection from sexually transmitted liver disease is the same as for all STDs: use condoms, use spermicides, use common sense when picking your sexual partners. Remember also that hepatitis can be passed through needles, including but not limited to those used in tattooing and body piercing.

I've been thinking about getting a tattoo, but I've heard you can get diseases from the needles they use, so now I'm apprehensive. How safe is getting a tattoo?

How safe is your tattoo artist? What kind of experience does he have? To what guidelines does he subscribe? What kind of equipment is being used? Is anything reused from one tattooee to the next? If so, how are they cleaned and sterilized (dipping in bourbon or holding over a match flame doesn't count)? These are the kinds of questions you should be asking before going under the needle. You can get HIV and Hepatitis B and C from reused needles, just to name two, and you can also get a host of other infections. I'd be making hard and pointed inquiries about how long the tattoo parlor has been in business. And I'd be asking for references from past clients. In fact, if it were my body part about to be illustrated, I'd want a brand-new, fresh, sealed, disposable needle that has never seen the underside of anyone else's epidermis.

There is also one other point to be aware of going in. While tattoos are no longer forever, they are certainly much more difficult and much more expensive to remove than they are to create. Be very sure you want your skin picture before you get it. One easy alternative is the temporary tattoo. No needles are used and the design is basically just applied to your skin like a decal — easy on, and easy off.

I read on the Internet recently that clinics across North America are paying men to participate in a safe-sex study. The catch is that you have to buy a book to get the address of the clinic in your city. Is this thing on the level?

Just because you read it on the Net does not mean it's true. Anybody can post anything they please on the newsgroups, which means some of the things you pick up there are valuable Net nuggets, and some are more like cyberpoop. I'm not saying you should trust no one, only that you should view the Net with healthy skepticism. There certainly are scientific studies that pay an honorarium to participants, but I know of no organization that acts as a broker or agent for those wishing to be subjects.

There's another reason to be cautious as well. When it comes to things sexual, the Internet can be a risky place to lurk. There are many unstable folks out there who have modems and ulterior motives, and pro surfers and newbies alike have good reason to tread softly on the keyboard when you don't know who's at the other end of the URL.

All told, this "safe-sex study" you read about sounds like a scam to me. If you'd like to participate in a legitimate research study, try calling your local universities. Many faculties are often in need of subjects.

Q My girlfriend and I have lived together faithfully for three years. Our sex life is fun and we enjoy our intimate moments, but I am very interested in having anal sex with her. She says that kind of activity results in AIDS. Is there any danger in anal sex between two faithful, heterosexual partners?

A There is no risk in transmitting AIDS in any sexual activity, as long as neither partner is HIV-positive. Anal intercourse is a high-risk activity for people who are HIV-positive, though, because a large amount of the virus is found in semen, and anal sex carries a high risk of creating tears or fissures in that area of the body. As a result, it's easier for the virus that causes AIDS to get into a new bloodstream, and infect a new victim. All of that is dependent, however, upon one of the two partners carrying the virus in the first place. If you don't have HIV, you can't give it to someone else. If anal sex is still a turn-on for you, and your girlfriend is willing, use good hygiene, a gentle technique, and plenty of lubrication.

7

Preg-NOT!

Studies have shown that over half of the babies born in North America each year are conceived by accident. My, isn't *that* a neat way to start your family — you had a great time in bed, and the by-product happened to be a child.

The great irony of conception is that it seems like those who don't want a baby get pregnant, while those who do, don't. Some women seem to get pregnant just by looking in the general direction of a male, while others don't conceive despite spending every waking hour in bed. On the average, it takes most couples six months to get pregnant after deciding to try, but many are still surprised to find that after the first attempt, nothing happened.

The list of ways to prevent pregnancy grows longer every year. Egg-preventing methods include the birth-control pill, contraceptive implants and injections, and the ultimate in ovulation prevention, tubal ligation surgery. The sperm-barrier methods include the old faithful condom, the big and clunky female condom, sponges, cervical caps, and diaphragms, all supplemented by spermicides, and the ultimate male preventative, the vasectomy.

 The companies that make birth-control devices are always talking about how effective their products are, and it's got me wondering about something. What is the chance of getting pregnant by having sex without any kind of birth control?

About the same as the chance of getting hit by a car while standing in the middle of a freeway on a moonless night wearing black clothes and a ski mask. In other words, you might get away safe, but is it a chance you really want to take?

How long do sperm live inside the body?

Let's face it: sperm are made to live inside the body, so it should come as no surprise that the little devils do quite well in there. Live sperm cells have been found nine and a half days after sex, hanging around the cervix like a payday crowd at a singles bar. Now, nine days may be a little extreme, but you can count on sperm living inside the female reproductive tract for at least five days, so unless you're trying to get pregnant, you'd better keep them out of there.

How long do sperm live outside the body?

 As hardy as they are in the womb, sperm cells fare much less well when exposed to the outside world. Most die within a few minutes, and even the strongest survive at most a few hours. Either way, be aware that while the odds may be low, it is still possible to get pregnant from sperm cells that have taken a detour to the great outdoors on their way to the egg.

 Are home pregnancy tests ever wrong?

 Yes and no. Home pregnancy tests look for the presence of human chorionic gonadotropin, a hormone that is secreted by the body only after conception. If you have just conceived, there may not be enough HCG in your urine to turn the little stick blue. This means if your test comes out negative, and you still think you're pregnant, you should do the test again a week or so later.

On the other hand, if the test shows you *are* pregnant, it is highly unlikely it is wrong. On rare occasions, people think they had a "false positive" because a silent miscarriage can happen in the very early stages of a pregnancy. The woman may think she just had a late and unusually heavy menstrual period. Keep in mind that if a home pregnancy test comes out positive, your next step should be a visit to your doctor anyway.

Ⓠ **Two weeks ago, I slept with my boyfriend. We didn't have intercourse, but we were close. I was nude and he had a pair of boxers on, he did have an orgasm, and now I'm a week late for my period. What are the chances I'm pregnant?**

Ⓐ The chances are probably minimal, but that does *not* mean boxer shorts are an effective replacement for a condom. Ms. Ovum doesn't care whether Mr. Sperm arrives under his own power or by express courier, as long as he gets there. Still, it's unlikely that any of them managed to make it through your boyfriend's boxer shorts and across the gulf dividing the two of you in bed. I know, to you it seemed like you were close together, but close is a relative term. When you have the perspective of a microscopic sperm cell, a half-inch becomes the Grand Canyon.

Unfortunately, you may still be pregnant, since it is much more likely some sperm could have found their way from his parts to yours on the tip of a finger. Still, don't panic yet. Your period may be late because you're stressed out over your close and unprotected encounter, or it may be delayed because your body is battling some kind of infection. You also may not be as regular as you thought, and you may simply be a week late for your period but *not* pregnant. There are many reasons for a period not to arrive on time. For peace of mind at a small price, pick up a home pregnancy test at your local drugstore, and be sure to follow the directions.

The bottom line for the women in the audience: please don't sit on the wet spot.

Ⓠ **There seem to be all kinds of birth control devices made for a woman's body, but only one for a man's (the condom), and I've always wondered why. I thought I had read about a male oral**

contraceptive being developed, but that seems like years ago. Is there a "pill" for men?

The answer to this one is yes and no. There's a group of people out there who think the lack of a male pill is some sort of conspiracy to keep women shackled to their fertility. Sorry to disappoint if you're one of them, but the real reason is pure mathematics. When it comes to the female pill, all the little tablet has to do is keep one little egg from taking a stroll down the Fallopian tubes each month. To design a pill for men, you must keep about 200 to 600 *million* sperm from launching a mass invasion.

That said, there are a couple of male contraceptives now undergoing testing. There have also been some promising results from China, and a study of an area where the men had abnormally low sperm counts. It seems the cooks of the region are fond of stir-frying in the oil of the gossypol plant, and that appears to keep sperm from forming. The simple male pill could be a takeout order away. Will it be as effective? Who knows? And lest we forget, no birth control pill will keep you from acquiring sexually transmitted diseases.

What exactly is this morning-after pill I keep hearing about, and why would you take it?

To put it simply, the morning-after pill is a high dose of hormones, roughly equivalent to taking a number of birth-control pills at the same time. (Unless your doctor tells you how many, do not try this!) It's used as a kind of emergency replacement when other birth-control methods may have failed, and it's called the morning-after pill because of when it's used — after sex, instead of before.

Fertilization of the human egg takes place in the Fallopian tubes, after release from the ovary. It then takes seventy-two hours to wind its way through the tubes to the uterus, where, if it attaches itself to the uterine wall, a fetus will begin developing. The morning-after pill keeps the fertilized egg from implanting itself in the uterine wall. No implantation, no pregnancy — it's as simple as that.

Most women who have used the morning-after pill have experienced some stomach trouble, so doctors typically prescribe an anti-nausea pill along with it — basically a motion-sickness remedy. You've probably guessed the main detraction to the morning-after pill by now: they're usable for seventy-two hours after sex and seventy-two hours *only*. After that, the fertilized egg is already out of the Fallopian tubes, no longer available for a detour away from the uterine wall. If your doctor's office is closed, call around to find a hospital emergency department or walk-in clinic that will dispense them for you. Don't wait. If you meet the time restriction, they are highly effective. If you miss the window, they're completely useless.

I can't stand condoms and my girlfriend gets sick from the pill, so she and I use the withdrawal method of birth control. How safe is this?

As they say in the banking world, there are penalties for early withdrawal, and the price could be much higher than simple dollars and cents. How safe is the withdrawal method? I've seen safer junk bonds. First, you have to consider that long before the male orgasm comes the pre-ejaculatory fluid — that drop or two you probably think is just nature's lubricant for men. In fact, that drop or two contains more than enough sperm to make you a daddy, and sperm couldn't care less whether they arrive in the womb at the beginning of sex or the end. Either way, they're happy to do their duty and fertilize. As a method of birth control, withdrawal makes a better method for uncontrolled birth. The stats say it has a 23-percent failure rate, which is like saying that every fourth time you use it, odds are you get pregnant.

There is, however, another reason why you might want to re-evaluate your technique here as well. Using the pull-out system, your entire focus during sex becomes "I'm having a good time, I'm having a good time — I better not blow it." How can you possibly relax and enjoy the moment when all of your attention is focused on when you're going to have your orgasm? More important, how can you relax and enjoy when you're worried you'll have your orgasm in the wrong location?

You are creating a geographical nightmare for yourself, and an unnecessary one at that. There are so many other easy and reliable birth-control methods available. Okay, all that said, here's my final word on the subject: if you absolutely will not consider any other method, better withdrawal than nothing at all. You still run the risk of conception, but the thousands of sperm present in your pre-ejaculatory fluid are still less risky than the hundreds of millions in the full male orgasm.

I am fifteen years old and I really, really, really want to get pregnant with my boyfriend. My best friend at school says I'm crazy — what do you think?

This may not be the worst idea you'll ever have, but when you're much older and looking back over your mistakes, I guarantee it would be right up there in the top five. I know people who were fifteen years old when they had their first child, and they all have regrets about it. In fact, I can give you the following advice from one of them, now a mother of two: "Becoming pregnant at fifteen will be neither fun nor romantic. What you will get out of the experience are stretch marks, loose sagging breasts, a funny line from your belly button to your bikini area, lost muscle tone, swelling of hands and feet, abnormal hair growth, back pain, and that pathetic teen mom look. You will feel isolated and lonely when your friends disappear. Your schooling will vanish. Dating and sex will become very difficult, and the father of your baby will probably disappear as well. The list goes on." To this perfect answer, let me add just a bit more food for thought: the book of famous, successful fifteen-year-old mothers is very, very thin.

My wife is pressuring me to have a vasectomy and I'm apprehensive about it. I've heard conflicting stories about the safety of the procedure. What's your take?

In the right hands, a vasectomy is a very safe operation. It is generally done under a local anesthetic by a urologist who probably performs dozens, if not hundreds, every year. It is, however, still surgery, and many men suffer at least some side effects after the snipping is done. These range from swelling of the testicles to infections, and while they can be painful, they are still considered minor problems. (Of course, I don't own testicles, so it's easy for me to call them "minor problems.")

The equivalent procedure on a woman is tubal ligation, commonly known as "having your tubes tied." This is a much more invasive and major procedure, done in a hospital operating room under general anesthetic. That is why it's easy for some women to argue to their mates that "your operation is safer than mine."

Safer it may be, but that's not the point: no one should pressure anyone into surgery, whether it's major or minor. The person who owns the body should decide where and when it gets cut. To help you make your own decision, you should consult your doctor to get the full medical perspective, as there are other long-term birth-control solutions that don't involve sterilization.

My boyfriend recently brought up the idea of anal sex, and I told him I'd think about it. The truth is, I'm kind of curious about it myself, but I need a couple of questions answered before I decide to give it a try. If a woman is using no contraception, can she become pregnant by anal sex? And is anal sex safe?

You can become pregnant, not by the anal sex itself but rather by the semen running down the small channel that separates the anal and vaginal openings. Sex doesn't cause pregnancy — the meeting of sperm and egg causes pregnancy. Rumor has it that U.S. soldiers in Vietnam sent their sperm home by military transport so their wives could start the family without them. The story may be untrue, but the method would have worked just fine, as long as the sperm were kept viable.

As for the safety of anal sex, there are three issues to consider. The first is that the tissues and muscles of that part of your body are not designed to accommodate large differences in size. Recent studies show that those who indulge in anal sex over a long period of time often find they develop a problem with incontinence. The second safety issue concerns whether a condom is used, since anal sex is the number-one transmission route for the AIDS virus. And third, you should never go from anal to vaginal sex without washing, as the micro-organisms that normally inhabit the two sites are not the same, and should not be carried from one place to the other.

My boyfriend says we don't need to use protection when I'm menstruating, because he says women are most fertile two weeks after their period, and not at all during it. Is this true?

A No, it is not. All women are fertile fourteen days *before* their *next* period, so it is only women with a twenty-eight-day cycle who are fertile precisely two weeks *after* their *last* period. Before you get too confused, keep in mind that women's cycles vary from about twenty-one days to about thirty. Day one of a woman's cycle is the first day of her period. So women on a twenty-one-day cycle will ovulate on day seven, and women on a thirty-day cycle would ovulate on day sixteen. All this means that different women are most fertile at different times of the month, which makes the rhythm system a much better method of starting a family than of pregnancy prevention.

As for whether a woman can get pregnant during her period, the answer is yes. Although the period is the sign that she did not conceive before, there's nothing to stop her from getting pregnant now, as she may ovulate in the near future. Sperm have been found living in the female reproductive tract for days after being deposited there. If a woman is on a short cycle, and has unprotected sex during her period, those sperm cells could still be viable to fertilize the next egg. And before you pull out the calendars and calculators, remember that many women have irregular cycles. Trying to calculate when they are most fertile becomes something like predicting the weather — guesswork at best, and not something to rely on for birth control.

Q **My girlfriend is three weeks late for her period, but she is not pregnant. We know that because she's taken three home pregnancy tests, and they've all come out negative. She is only seventeen, and under a lot of stress. Could this be why her period is late?**

A There can be many reasons why she's late, ranging from illness to stress to, of course, pregnancy. Assuming you followed the instructions on the three test packages and she's *not* expecting, the missed period could be one of nature's ways of protecting its investment. In survival terms, a sick or stressed mother is not exactly a good host for a fetus, so Mother Nature sometimes dodges the possibility by interrupting a woman's monthly cycle. The interruption keeps pregnancy from happening, and also causes the woman to skip one or more periods. Deal with the stress, and her periods may come back, but she should check with her doctor in any case, to be both certain and safe.

Q **My husband and I have had our kids (two girls and a boy, all lovely, intelligent, and talented, thanks for asking). Now we're trying to decide on our birth control, and since we don't want any more children, we're considering the permanent options. What are the chances of getting pregnant after a tubal ligation or vasectomy?**

A We've all heard the horror stories, or read them in the newspaper: a woman goes in to get her tubes tied, and three months or five years later, she's pregnant again. It just goes to show how amazing those little ova are, and how determined they are to find a way to meet up with a nice new sperm. Seriously, though, the chance of a tubal ligation spontaneously reversing itself is mighty slim. Even when a woman wants to change her mind after the operation, it takes another surgery to reattach the severed ends, and there's only about a 50-50 chance that the reversal will be a success.

Much the same can be said of vasectomies and their reversals. Sometimes they can be undone, sometimes they can't, and sometimes the ends of the snipped vas deferens miraculously find each other and recon-nect. This, of course, leads to another surprise pregnancy to be reported in the tabloids. It's possible in some cases that the vasectomy was not suc-cessful in the first place, which is why men who have them are supposed to have sperm counts done for a period of time after the surgery.

Put simply, you should consider any surgical sterilization to be a per-manent, irreversible procedure that, like so many other methods of birth control, is not absolutely, positively, 100-percent foolproof.

I'm eighteen years old and thinking of going on the pill, but I don't want my parents to find out. Is there a way I can be sure my doctor won't tell them?

If you're old enough to have sex, then you're certainly old enough to use birth control. If you're mature enough for the adult activ-ity that is sex with all its complications, then you should also be able to handle the possibility that your parents will discover you are sexually active. No matter how careful or secretive you are, the chance exists that they'll find out. If you feel okay about having a sex life, you should have some response for them if and when they do.

That said, the absolute confidentiality of your doctor visits will depend on where you live, and who your physician is. If you reside in a state or province where age eighteen is legal adulthood, then your doctor is legally and ethically obliged to keep everything about your visits strict-ly confidential. If you live in a place where being eighteen means you are still legally a minor, then it depends on the physician. What you can do in that case is to call your doctor, tell him or her that you have some private business to discuss, and ask whether he or she will feel compelled to share the information with your parents. If you can't get at least a verbal assurance of privacy from your doctor, you can shop around until you find one who will agree to the request. Your other option is to find a youth clinic, where your confidentiality will be assured.

 My girlfriend says she read somewhere that a woman can't get pregnant unless she has an orgasm. Is this true?

A Most definitely not. The egg has no idea whether the earth is moving for you, or if you're just gazing at the ceiling, trying to decide what color to paint it. This is a myth that comes out of the theory that the rhythmic vaginal contractions of a woman's orgasm help the sperm on their way to the ovum. If it is proven to be true, then the female orgasm could be said to *aid* conception, but it would in no way mean that the lack of an orgasm would *prevent* conception.

Is douching an effective means of birth control?

A No, it is an extremely *in*effective method of birth control. Consider the situation here: the sperm are trying to get upstream to the cervix, so when you douche, you're just giving them a hand — think of it as river rafting for sperm.

My husband and I have been trying to get pregnant for a while now without any luck. Is it true that his choice of underwear could have something to do with it?

A Yes, it could. A man's testicles hang away from his body because they require a temperature a few points below the rest of the body in order to maximize sperm production. That's why in the tropical heat they actually hang lower to catch the cooling breezes, while in the cold of winter, they get pulled up toward the body for added warmth. Wearing bikini underwear is like wrapping a sweater around your testicles — the briefs pull them into the body where cool air can't circulate around the scrotum, and the added warmth can cut down the sperm count. If you're trying to get pregnant and your spouse is fond of briefs, do yourselves a favor and buy him some boxers. For the same reasons, he should stay away from hot tubs if you're trying to get pregnant.

Q **A friend of mine recently had a baby, and she told me one of the extra bonuses is that she and her husband won't need to use condoms until she finishes nursing. Is it true that breastfeeding protects you from getting pregnant?**

A It's true that most women don't start ovulating immediately after childbirth if they are breastfeeding, but the key word here is "most." While the hormonal balance of a nursing mother may appear to provide the same effect as the pill, it is not a sure thing, and many a breastfeeding mother has found herself once again pregnant, long before she was ready. A further complication here is that if you do conceive, you will be advised by your doctor to stop breastfeeding immediately, regardless of how long you had planned to nurse the baby. Unless you're really ready for "two in diapers," I'd use one or more of the more reliable methods of birth control as soon as you resume your sex life.

Q My husband and I have been happily married for ten years now, and we've tried every birth control method known to mankind. We really don't want to have kids now, but we might later on, so we don't want to do anything permanent. Is there any way we can forsake the jellies, latex, and/or chemicals and still be reasonably sure I won't get pregnant?

A Your nearest birth-control clinic can run through the natural family planning methods available to you. Don't be surprised when you leave the premises armed with graphs, charts, and an ovulation thermometer, but at least you won't have a bag full of creams and devices. Once you get home, you will be embarking on a regime of checking your cervix, taking your temperature, and charting the resulting days of the month during which you must abstain from intercourse. As you can imagine, you'll have to be highly motivated and patient to be successful with this less-than-carefree method.

Q My girlfriend just went on the pill. How long before I can kiss the condoms goodbye?

A Many doctors say the birth-control pill is effective at the end of the first week — some even think it's probably effective after the third or fourth pill. Rather than play with the statistics, I'd suggest you continue using condoms through the entire first month's cycle of birth-control pills. Even if the pill is already doing its job, taking one every day is a brand-new part of her routine — the habit is not ingrained yet. If she forgets one or more in the first month, the condoms are still there as a backup.

One last point to remember is that the pill is a one-trick pony: it prevents pregnancy, but that's it. A condom, on the other hand, is a birth-control device and STD preventer in one package. Before eliminating this extra protection, be sure neither you nor your partner is carrying any unwanted viral or bacterial company on your person.

My friend tells me my IUD can interfere with radio signals, like the ones that run garage-door openers or remote controls. Is this true?

Does your TV set flip over to channel 57 every time you hop into bed? Does the neighbor's car alarm go off every time you have sex standing up? No? Well, there, then. And one more thing — it won't set off the metal detector at the airport either. ("Please put your birth-control devices and pocket change into this tray, and step through the arch" — I don't think so!)

8

Wrapping Your Package

Barrier devices have probably been around as long as sex itself, from Dr. Condom, who invented the sheath that bears his name, to Casanova, who used hollowed-out lemon halves, and back to Cleopatra, who employed honey and crocodile dung. People will always be searching for devices that allow the most fun with the least inconvenience, and the fewest unwanted pregnancies and diseases. Millions of dollars continue to go into research on designs for things that will minimize the interference and maximize the contact between two people. Ironically, most of the products the hardware engineers come up with seem to be merely new twists on the oldest idea: wrapping your package to keep yours and your partner's apart. The good old condom, tried and true, is not entirely fail-safe, but it's the only double-duty prophylactic, preventing pregnancy and the transmission of disease at the same time.

Q I've seen many brands of lubricants on the market, but only one that is also a spermicide. I'd like to know how much more protection one receives when using a spermicidal lubricant with a condom, as opposed to just a condom. Also, do plain lubricants offer any additional protection?

A Plain lubricants do not offer any additional direct protection, although indirectly they may — all lubricants will help ensure the condom itself doesn't tear. The only condom worth using is the one in working order, and any puncture, however small, makes a condom worth less than its weight in latex.

There are, however, definite direct advantages to using spermicidal lubricants on both the inside and outside surfaces of the condom: no conception can occur if the sperm don't show up for the party.

Q My sister's new boyfriend claims he can't use condoms because he's allergic to the latex. Can you really be allergic to condoms? And if so, what are the reactions?

A The good news is, more and more people are using condoms to prevent the spread of disease and unwanted pregnancy. The bad news is, more and more people seem to be developing allergies to the latex used in the creation of condoms. It's a trend also visible in the medical world in general, where doctors, nurses, dentists, and the like have upped their use of latex gloves. The symptoms may include a rash or itching or general latent discomfort. What can you do if you become sensitive to latex? Try one of the new polyurethane-based condoms if you can find them, or layer a lambskin condom under or over the latex one (depending on which partner is allergic).

The other item that can cause an allergy to develop is the chemical nonoxynol-9, commonly known as spermicide. Your best alternative is to use condoms which don't contain spermicide in the lubrication. Unfortunately, this lowers the effectiveness of the condom in preventing pregnancy.

This has been bugging me for years, so I'm turning to you for an opinion. Do you think it's fair that the guy usually has to get the condoms?

Well, if it were true, it would not be fair, but as it turns out, it isn't true. In fact, most everywhere you look these days, half or more of the condoms sold are bought by women. This is a good idea for several reasons, besides the fact that women should pay for half of the protection when they're having half the fun (in theory, anyway). More important, a condom is a very cheap life preserver. When you consider what women spend on cosmetics every month, it's positively dirt cheap. Still, condoms are *relatively* expensive, when you compare them with other items made from latex. Why are surgical gloves two cents a pair and condoms a buck each? Is *that* fair? I think not.

Are there any condoms that are 100-percent effective in preventing pregnancy and disease? And how do they test them, anyway?

A Condoms are tested in a variety of ways. They are filled with air to see how far they can be inflated before they burst (the pressure test), and they are filled with water to see if there are any pinholes (the leak test). In the lab, many condoms test out to 99- or 100-percent reliability, but the real-life effective rate depends on a lot more than the integrity of manufacture and the grade of latex. What really matters is whether the end-user (so to speak) has a ragged fingernail that will tear the condom as he puts it on; whether she left it in her purse with a pierced earring; whether he put it on at the right moment; whether he took it off properly; and how long it sat in the back of his wallet before he got around to using it.

Like milk cartons, cold remedies, and everything else these days, condoms have an expiry date — they're best used when fresh from the factory. If you want to know the annual ratings on different condom brands, you can check the consumer publications that print them each year. Also not recommended are loose condoms sold singly and found on the drugstore counter, where they can be punctured by delinquent idiots looking to spoil your fun in a big way. Remember, though, it's just as important how you use the ones you finally buy.

Q I know you're supposed to use condoms to keep from getting disease, but I also know that condoms are not even perfect as birth control. So I guess my question is, how good are they, exactly? What's the chance of becoming pregnant or getting AIDS, if you do use a condom?

A A condom is never 100-percent effective, so you should never rely on one as your only line of defense, or even your *first* line of defense, for that matter. The first should be your intelligence — your brain. The questions you need to ask yourself are, who is this person I am with, and what do I know about him/her? Having answered those questions to your satisfaction, the second line of defense is to rubberize. That way, you make sure your risk is as low as possible — even if your partner was a good liar.

Your chances of contracting AIDS multiply each time you have unprotected intercourse. If you already made the mistake once, don't think there's no longer any point in protecting yourself. Some experts say a woman has a 10-percent chance of getting AIDS each time she has unprotected sex with an HIV-positive man. That means you may be lucky enough to escape unscathed the first few times, but sooner or later, your luck will run out.

Q **My best friend told me she was having sex with her boyfriend the other night, and afterward she realized the condom had ruptured at the end. I find myself worrying now about the next time my own boyfriend and I get together, so I figure if I feel more prepared, I'll be less tense. Tell me — what should you do if the condom breaks while you're having sex?**

A Me? I'd probably jump up immediately and let gravity assist. I don't know if it would really help prevent pregnancy, but it would probably keep me from panicking.

Seriously, though, it's better to be prepared beforehand for this very emergency. Hopefully you were using some backup method like a spermicide, in which case you should pump in another plungerful right away. If you weren't, you hopefully have some around, where you can get to it in a big hurry. Finally, if you suspect there's any chance at all you may be ovulating when the break occurs, you have a seventy-two-hour window in which to get the morning-after pill from your doctor or family planning clinic.

Q I think I'm a responsible, caring, '90s kind of guy. I care about preventing the spread of disease and not getting my girlfriend pregnant. So please tell me why it is that every time I put on a condom, I seem to wilt.

A It's probably because the idea of latex conjures up sterile kinds of images in your mind. It seems more like a medical thing to do than an erotic thing to do. If you're just beginning your sex life, the best way to make friends with your condoms is probably just to use them each and every time. That way, you'll build the association in your mind that sex equals condoms, rather than sex plus condoms equals system crash.

If you're already well into your sexual life and the problem has now arisen (so to speak), the stumbling block may be your brain concluding that condoms equal disease. The answer here is to eliminate the possibility that the condom is covering a disease carrier in the first place (get tested). After that, the condom will merely become a vital link in the sexual equation.

The best answer for this problem, however it has come about, is to eroticize your condom. Make it sexy, or better yet, make it a sex toy. Experiment with different brands — modern condoms come in a variety of thicknesses, sizes, and widths, and many men prefer the ultra-thin types. If you wilt when you don your condom, get your partner to dress you for succex (sorry) instead. Also, don't keep your condom in the sock drawer down the hall across from the bathroom, or you'll have to take a foreplay intermission to find your little buddy. Instead, take it out of the wrapper and arrange it business side up on the bedside table, just before you begin the festivities. That way, you'll be able to slip into your "something comfortable" at the appropriate moment, without interrupting the flow.

A buddy of mine insists he's better protected from AIDS because he uses two condoms at a time when he's having sex. Does layering condoms one on top of the other really give you twice the protection of just one?

Double-bagging is probably not that helpful. It's much more important to make sure the single condom you use is used properly, and that you back it up with some other method, like spermicide on the inside and outside. Also, remember that it's just as important to know who you're having sex with, before you worry about the accoutrements of sex itself. Knowing your partner means you can better evaluate the likelihood that they're putting you at risk, and therefore keep the risk as small as possible. No number of condoms worn simultaneously will save you from disaster if you haven't protected yourself before sex even becomes an issue.

**Are lambskin condoms safe?**

No, they aren't, if you're worried about STDs. These condoms are actually made from sheep innards, and were once the elite product of male birth control. The reason is that they conduct heat more readily than latex, and so promise more realistic sensations for the man during intercourse.

Whether that claim is true or not is beside the point. Lambskin condoms are *unsafe* because of the material itself. The pores of a lambskin condom are small enough to prevent the transmission of sperm cells, but large enough for viruses like HIV to penetrate. This means that using these types of condoms may prevent pregnancy, but they won't save you from sexually transmitted diseases, like AIDS.

My boyfriend bought some unlubricated condoms by mistake the other day, so now he says he'll just use some Vaseline with them. Is this a good idea?

Never, *ever* use petroleum- or oil-based substances with a condom — they act as solvents and will start dissolving the latex as soon as the two substances come in contact. If you need more friction-eviction, always use water-based lubricants like K-Y Jelly. You should find them in the same drugstore aisle where the condoms are kept, but if they're not there, just ask the pharmacist. Better yet, pick up a spermicide — you'll get added protection against disease and unwanted pregnancy, and all spermicides come in a water-based solution.

One more thing while we're on the topic: this same warning applies to any other solution that is oil-based, such as the skin creams and lotions you may be using for moisturizing your skin or giving each other a massage. If you are using any of these creams, keep them away from your private parts, and be sure to wash your hands before handling your condoms.

9

Sex and Drugs
(Rock and Roll Optional)

Some people look to chemistry in their quest for the ultimate sexual experience. The idea seems to be that there's a better sex life out there, and some combination of alcohol or drugs or whatever will give it to them. Ironically, the substances ingested in the hunt for perfect sex will often make sex unlikely if not impossible.

For others, drugs and alcohol are the means to overcome shyness or low self-esteem, while still others lean on chemicals as a way to get past their own reluctance to have sex. There are all kinds of people who probably shouldn't be sexually active: they're the ones getting stoned first, so they can convince themselves they're having a good time. Ultimately, these strategies have a way of catching up with you, because the shyness or low self-esteem or whatever is still there, and you can't be drugged out all the time.

Then there are the mystical, mythical sex drugs: aphrodisiacs. There will always be people who believe that somewhere out there in the jungle, like the fountain of youth, there's a magic love potion that will arouse the flames of passion. No one's ever found one, and there's an ever-growing body of evidence to the contrary, but facts will never dissuade some dreamers from their illusions. Perhaps ironically enough, while no one has been able to find a drug to rev up the sex drive, there are some that will make it sputter to a halt, generally as an unwanted side effect. These include some of the drugs used to treat high blood pressure, diabetes, or depression.

How does alcohol affect your sex drive?

About the same way running out of gas affects the car you drive: it makes your equipment stop purring and start sputtering. Eventually, it stops altogether. Alcohol affects the circulatory system — your internal blood flow. Unfortunately, the status of the penis is controlled by blood flow. Send more blood in, you get an erection; lower the blood pressure, lose the erection. A recent study of male impotence found that most men who have trouble in that department smoke, drink, or do both.

There are some indications from American and European studies that a glass or two of wine a day can actually be good for you, however, which would explain why the average French citizen has less heart trouble than the average North American. Before you take off for the wine store, though, remember that anything more than a glass or two a day is definitely a major health risk. Aside from impotence, liver trouble, and heart problems, drinking too much hard liquor can cause breast growth in men. This is because of an increased production of estrogen, one of the so-called female hormones.

My friend says the caffeine in coffee increases your sex drive, but I find it just makes me jittery and turns me off. Who's right here?

You both are. Caffeine is one of those substances that seem to affect different people in different ways. You may be bouncing off the walls after one cup, others can down a pot and a half and go right to sleep. If your friend thinks it's a turn-on, she should go right ahead and use it as one. Obviously, it's not for you, and that's fine. Some people like satin sheets, others hate them. Some women like tall guys, others go for short. There is no one sure-fire answer that constitutes the magic formula for romance. If there were, it would be on sale in every department store in the world, and it would be really expensive.

I've heard that if a girl takes the pill, her breasts get bigger. If I were to take the pill, would it increase the size of my penis?

No. However, it will probably increase the size of your breasts, so you can start sharing your girlfriend's bras. The pill is made up of female hormones, and it should not be put into the male body.

What are the effects of Ecstasy, and how does it affect sexual pleasure?

A Ecstasy is one of the so-called designer drugs, originally derived from the amphetamine family generally called speed. Users of this drug experience a feeling of euphoria — hence the name. As for its effects on sexual pleasure, while most users report feelings of love toward their partners, most find the idea of sex under its influence either too silly to contemplate, or just plain physically impossible. In fact, some people on Ecstasy fall in love with everything around them — tables, chairs, houseplants, and that moldy, leftover tuna casserole. As you can imagine, any man or woman thrown into that situation as an object of desire would face a lot of stiff competition, even if it came from inanimate objects.

Q **I met this girl a month ago in a club, and since then, we've probably spent about twelve nights together. All of those nights have started in one club or another, and she likes to drink, so all of our sex so far has taken place while she was at least a little drunk. I'd really like to find out what it would be like to make love when she's sober, but I'm afraid if I bring it up, she'll get upset. What should I do?**

A Bring it up — in conversation, that is. First of all, in some of the United States and all of Canada, having sex with a person who is bombed is considered sexual assault, consent under the influence notwithstanding. Second, if all your lovemaking has happened while she's intoxicated, then you really don't know who it is you're having sex with — or whether she even knows she's having sex.

You say you're afraid she'll get upset if you bring it up. Maybe it's better if she *does* get upset, since this kind of behavior isn't very healthy for either of you. When you talk to her about her drinking problem, she may thank you, or she may curse you — either way, at least you'll find out who she is. And two more things — need I say them? Be sure she's sober when you have your talk, and be sure she's sober the next time you have sex.

I just found out a guy I know is using cocaine, and using it quite often. How can I talk to my friend about his drug problem without sounding like I'm lecturing him?

Unfortunately, a drug problem often becomes a relationship problem, too. This is because the person often does the drugs around you, or shows up after having done the drugs. That makes their problem yours as well. If you are uncomfortable with this, you have to tell your friend that his drug use doesn't work for you. You can't tell him he should stop using drugs, because no one ever changes their behavior until they are ready. You can say, "I am not comfortable being around people who are stoned. I will not be in a relationship with a person who is carrying or doing drugs. I'm sorry, but should that situation change, you can let me know." That's the scenario for a friend.

If, on the other hand, this is a person you are very close to, someone who is a significant part of your life, then perhaps you can be part of his support structure to get rid of the problem. You can let him know what circumstances will allow you to be there for him. For example, you'll be there if he's in a rehab program. Be careful, though, that you don't end up becoming his driver, sole support person, and the one who saves him from the results of his doing drugs. Like alcoholism, drug dependency is a problem that sometimes creates helpers who have bigger problems than the addict himself.

Q I've heard there's some kind of prescription drug that gives you an orgasm when you yawn. Is this for real? If so, how does it work? And where can I get some? Just kidding on the last one.

A The rumor you've heard has probably been misquoted, another fine example of the broken-telephone system of a story going from one person to another, and changing in the process. There is a drug that has been specifically designed for men suffering impotence with psychological causes. When placed under the tongue, the pill will give the man an erection that lasts for about an hour. One side effect of this pill is that many men find it also makes them yawn. It causes the erection and often the yawn; it does *not* cause an orgasm *when* you yawn. The other part of this newly popular urban myth is the rumor that the drug in question is sold in some countries as an over-the-counter cold remedy. The actual drug is dispensed by prescription only, and it is *not* an antihistamine.

Q I want to know what you know about aphrodisiacs, please. Don't hold back.

A What I can tell you about aphrodisiacs is that most of them are in your mind — and I mean that literally. If you believe that having daffodils in a jar next to your bed will make you the next of the red-hot lovers, then that's probably what will happen. Doctors call it the placebo effect.

Through the ages, at one time or another, just about every substance and/or technique has been touted as an aphrodisiac. One medieval prescription involved holding an apple under your arm until it got sweaty, then having your unsuspecting partner eat the fruit. I find it hard to believe that would get anyone to fling their clothes off, and it's rather unappetizing, too. Other items believed over the years to stimulate desire have included beans, lentils, beets, carrots, and turnips, all of which will create heat only if you put them in a soup. Mandrake root and ginseng have been listed as well, probably because they resemble the human body in a weird and twisted way. Chocolate and alcohol have been on the top-ten list for ages: chocolate because it apparently releases the chemical in the brain that is associated with pleasure, alcohol because it helps loosen inhibitions in small quantities. Of course, too much chocolate or alcohol isn't the best thing, either.

Despite fervent and meticulous searches over the centuries, the simple, effective aphrodisiac remains as elusive a quarry as the Loch Ness Monster. Sure, they may find it at some point in the future, but don't hold your breath waiting for the announcement.

It seems there are dozens of ads in the magazines for colognes guaranteed to attract the opposite sex. The whole thing looks bogus to me, but there are so many of them, I'm starting to wonder. Are any of them real?

I wouldn't spend my retirement savings on any of them, but there is some indication that our olfactory sense plays a bigger role in mutual attraction than experts once thought. In one study, a group of women were given a bunch of unwashed T-shirts, and they had no trouble picking out which one had been worn by their own mates, using only their sense of smell. Another study seemed to show that people are unlikely to be attracted if they don't like each other's natural body odor.

Pheromones were once believed to play a role in mating only in lower animals and insects, but most experts now think they have some role in human attraction as well. Despite all this, however, there is no evidence that any commercial manufacturer has so far found the magic scent to make women flock to your side.

 I am using steroids to help get my muscle bulk up. Are there any side effects that will affect my sex life?

Yes, there are, many of them, including the possibility that your testicles will shrink to the size of peanuts. Your body may also stop producing the natural hormones that the steroids mimic, so you could end up with the loss of your body hair, a change in your voice from bass or tenor to alto or soprano, enlarged breasts, sterility, impotence, and who knows, maybe even cancer. There are reasons why steroid use is banned from athletic events, and it's more than unfair competition. Steroids do bad things to your body, and the longer you use them, the worse off you'll end up.

Is it true that Vitamin E is good for your sex drive?

There is no evidence that any vitamin, mineral, or nutritional supplement will boost your sex drive. Perhaps the one exception is the extreme case, where you are suffering from such malnutrition that you have no sex drive at all. The bottom line is that a healthy diet provides all the vitamins the human body needs, and some, including Vitamin E, can be toxic if taken in too great a quantity.

10

The Male Unit

Men and women will always be different creatures, and part of the reason is the way their bodies are constructed. His genitals are located down in front of him, where he can never get away from them. If he sits down, they sit down with him. He goes for a walk, he takes them with. He gets in a bath, they float (all right, some of them float). If he stands at attention and lets his arms dangle to their normal extended length, guess what ends up at the same level as the palms of his hands? Because of all this, boy babies tend to find their equipment sooner than girl babies (more on them later).

The male unit also affects the male psyche, because of the change-able nature of the equipment. A penis starts off rather small, only to grow much larger, in most boys, at the onset of puberty. Penises also come in varying sizes from one man to the next, and it's impossible to tell from their dimensions in the resting state what size they will be in the condition of arousal. In fact, larger resting penises tend to grow little when erect, while those that are smaller in their resting state tend to grow more. This means that two units that are totally different to begin with can end up exactly the same size.

Once little boys discover their own equipment, they tend to compare it with Daddy's. He looks at his little thing hanging way down there below him, then up at the enormous thing dangling just overhead and thinks, "Oh my goodness, mine is so tiny." Never mind that anything overhead always looks bigger than something down below. Never mind that he's four or five years old and Daddy is thirty. Never mind that his will still get bigger and Daddy's won't. All he thinks is, "I'm a little boy, my daddy has a bigger one than me," and it's a thought that will never leave his head for the rest of his life.

I need to know how to get my boyfriend to last longer during sex. Is there something I can do to get him to hold out for five or ten minutes?

Five or ten minutes? Believe it or not, some guys actually go longer than that. Unfortunately, for some other men, five minutes might as well be a year, if you know what I mean.

Anyway, back to your question. I can't help you if you're looking for a quick fix, but if you're willing to invest a few dollars, and your guy can put in about six weeks of work, I may be able to point you in the right direction. Head on down to your favorite bookstore and pick up *The New Male Sexuality* by Dr. Bernie Zilbergeld. If you faithfully follow his exercises for six weeks, Dr. Z. says you'll get results.

One thing I can assure you: male premature orgasm is a problem that is nearly 100-percent repairable. Usually the owner of the equipment is out of touch with the feelings in his body that are mounting toward orgasm. In other words, his body is in free fall, and he has to find the rip cord on the parachute and get more in tune with how fast the ground is approaching.

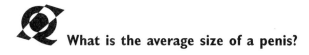 **My boyfriend tells me it is better for his health to have regular sex, and he says once a day is a minimum. Is it true the fluids flow better if he orgasms every day?**

I think not. His penis is not a drawbridge: it requires no regular oiling to keep it rising and falling smoothly. It will go up and down just fine, regardless of whether it is put into use on a daily, weekly, monthly, or yearly basis. The male body supplies adequate blood to that part of the body regardless of the opportunity for actual sex, probably another reason why men have erections at the worst times, in the strangest places, including in the middle of the night when they're fast asleep.

Still, there is something to be said for sex and health being related in a general way for both men and women. Some studies have shown that people enjoying satisfactory sex lives have healthier attitudes, and live longer, too. Sex is probably one of the best, most inexpensive, chemical-free, readily obtainable stress relievers known to humankind. Of course, that last sentence would be contradicted if you were having unsafe sex with the wrong person, so please don't take it as a blanket recommendation to jump between the sheets with the next bicycle courier who rings your doorbell.

What is the average size of a penis?

A The average erect penis is five and three-quarter inches long — about the size of a Mars bar. According to the research, 90 percent of North American men have non-erect penises ranging from three to five inches in length, with the average relaxed penis coming out at about four inches. Coincidentally, four inches is also the average circumference, with 93 percent of North American male units measuring between three and five inches around. However, any man's nesting penis size can vary from one time period to the next, depending on things like weather conditions. As any guy who's climbed out of a swimming pool on a cold day can tell you, if you're shivering, it's probably shrinking. Also, the resting size can vary depending on whether the penis in question has been involved in recent sexual activity. For some time after arousal, some amount of blood remains in the equipment — not enough to keep it erect, but enough to keep it from getting back to its completely resting state.

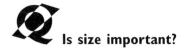

Is size important?

A Whether you are hung like a hamster or a killer whale, you are still a mammal, and whether you consider yourself a high-rise or a three-story walkup, there are no prizes for the biggest unit. Most women don't care how big a penis is, unless of course it is extremely large, and in contrast to the dialogue in blue movies, most women find an enormous penis frightening, not exciting. I've heard from many women that they were intimidated by their boyfriend's overendowment — I've heard from very few that their boyfriends were too small.

The whole issue of size seems to be much more a "guy thing," possibly because, as mentioned, a man's equipment hangs out there where they can't help but notice it, and where they can't help but compare it with the others they see in the locker room. If you're concerned about your size, keep in mind that a flaccid penis gives little indication how large it will become when erect. Also, remember that only the first third of a woman's vagina has any abundance of nerve cells to stimulate, so as far as a woman's pleasure goes, anything more than about three inches is just so much surplus joystick.

I understand there are some surgical methods to enlarge the penis. Can you tell me the differences between them?

First, I suggest you read the answer to the last question. Anyway, here goes. There are three main methods to enlarge the penis currently in use, none of which I would have done, if I had a penis to begin with.

The first is not really an enlargement at all, but rather an operation that partially frees the root of the penis from its anchorage in the pubic bone. Part of the penis is normally inside the body, but this procedure allows more of it to protrude in front of you, instead of remaining tucked away inside. Personally, I figure if a part of all penises is anchored inside the body, there's probably a good reason. Pushing it outside for the sake of an extra inch seems like a scary idea to me, regardless of how many plastic surgeons say it's safe to do so.

Another enlargement surgery involves the implantation of fat or other tissue into the penis, thereby enhancing what you already have. Some men think this is wonderful. There is also a method of penile augmentation that doesn't affect the length but does make your unit wider.

There has been a lot of controversy over all of these procedures, most significantly over whether the extra quarter-inch to one inch obtained really makes more than a psychological difference to any man. Also, any surgical procedure involving the use of general anesthesia has a risk of its own, simply because of the anesthetic itself. People have died from complications that had nothing directly to do with the procedure — including procedures to add an inch to a penis.

I have a large penis and I find it awkward and embarrassing. What should I do?

You may as well get used to it, because short of finding a genie to grant your three biggest wishes, you're going to have it for the rest of your life. Large penises have developed a certain mystique thanks to their prominence in X-rated movies, where they are generally attached to actors with names like "Long John Armstrong." In reality, very large penises cause their owners more grief than joy. Most overendowed men find that technique becomes much more important, and they can get away with less than their more average-sized peers. Many women are intimidated by a very large man, while others find his lap toy stimulating.

My current boyfriend is in his forties and hasn't been to a doctor in about twenty years. I've read that men in that age group should have annual checkups because of things like prostate problems, but he tells me he feels fine and doesn't need a physical. Why is it men seem to have such a thing about going to the doctor?

Men and women do seem to have large differences in their attitudes toward the medical profession, particularly when it comes to their sexual equipment. Women know that as much as they may hate the dreaded internal exam, they must go. So it is that every year, they thump down to their doctor and put on that ridiculous paper smock. Then they climb up on a table covered with cold construction paper, and assume the most undignified position imaginable — legs raised and feet parted in stirrups. Next, the doctor puts his face about five inches from their genitals, and starts poking around. As bad as it sounds, guys, the reality is even worse. Nevertheless, women resign themselves that it's all part of the dues that must be paid in the Female Club.

Men, on the other hand, hardly ever have their equipment examined by their family practitioner — and almost never on a routine basis. As a result, they're often reluctant and self-conscious when it's time to whip their units out for inspection, and it's unfortunately become a factor in the way sexually transmitted diseases are passed around. Most women may be embarrassed about getting undressed and being examined, but it doesn't stop them from going. Many men, on the other hand, procrastinate endlessly about that visit to the doctor, even when they suspect something has gone awry with their equipment. They know they should get it checked out, but first, their fear of infection has to do battle with the discomfort of making the appointment.

The whole dynamic is compounded by the sporadic nature of male medical visits. A woman has a regular yearly opportunity to say, "By the way, I've been wondering what this bump is..." A man has to call for an appointment, and often gets asked by a female nurse at the other end to describe his current problem.

There's one more reason why women should actually feel a bit of empathy for the males of the species. We have to get used to the oh-so-personal internal exam from a young age, so we do. Imagine the shock that awaits the man when it's time for his first prostate examination, otherwise known as a digital rectal exam. Imagine the further shock when it dawns on him that he'll have to have one every year for the rest of his life.

I've slept with five different men in my lifetime so far, and they all had one thing in common that frustrated me no end. Can you please tell me why men always seem to fall asleep after sex?

You have your choice here of either science or cynicism. The cynical view is that men are really shallow beings who are only interested in sex for the sake of sex — once they've had their way, they really have no further use for you, so falling asleep is a way of ending their interaction with you. Like I said, cynical.

The scientific view is that the whole thing is an evolutionary enigma having to do with hormones. The latest research seems to show that in men, the orgasm triggers the release of a sleep-inducing chemical in the brain. Perhaps this has something to do with our ancient ancestors only having sex when there were no saber-toothed tigers around who might eat them. After sex, they just feel so comfy and safe, they can drop off to sleep, and the chemical release evolved to assist the process. Whatever.

The enigma I mentioned earlier is that the brains of women do *not* release this chemical after sex. In fact, in women, the brain releases a chemical after orgasm that does the exact opposite: it wakes them up. As a result, in beds around the world, the sex act is followed most often by the sight of a woman staring at the ceiling, pondering the future, and a man curled up beside her, fast asleep, and possibly snoring. What evolutionary advantage could be won by this combination? I have no idea. Maybe we'll get to it in the next edition of this book, if the scientists can make up their minds by then.

Why does one of my testicles hang lower than the other?

A Probably because if they hung at precisely the same level, they'd clunk together when you walk.

Your testicles hang at different levels for the same reason your feet are different sizes — contrary to common belief, the human body is not symmetrical. Your left and right sides are different from your eyes to your toes; it's just that the differences are usually too slight to notice. This asymmetry is why most people say they don't look like themselves in photographs. The face you see in the mirror is reversed by the process of reflection — the one you see in the snapshot is the "real" you — the you other people see.

Why do men notice their testicles hang differently but don't notice that their ears hang differently? Probably because men pay more attention to their testes than their ears. And one more thing, for you trivia buffs: usually it's the left one that hangs lower. I have no idea why that is true, it just is. And don't worry if you find that on your body, it's the right one — it really doesn't matter.

Q I'm a twenty-two-year-old male with an embarrassing problem. When erect, my penis curves to the left. Is this a problem? And if so, is there any type of surgery available to cure it?

A No, it's normal. In fact, it would be abnormal if your penis pointed straight as an arrow at a 90-degree angle from your body, in a direct line to the magnetic north pole. According to the Kinsey Report on sex, 30 percent of male penises curve to the left, while only 5 per cent point straight down. Normal penises curve right, left, up, and down. There is nothing to worry about, unless your particular slant on things is causing problems during intercourse, or you wish to use your joystick to shoot pool, or in the rare case that the deviation is so extreme as to be physically uncomfortable or painful.

There are a couple of medical conditions that may cause a change in direction later in life, so if your curvature of the spire has only recently appeared, check with your doctor. Other than those few conditions, it's usually just a case of a penis curving whichever way it likes. And no, this is not caused by using the left hand when going solo, and cannot be corrected by changing hands.

Q **I'm in very good health, with one small exception — one of my testicles is really sore. What could this be?**

A Sore testicles usually have one of three causes. If you're in your early twenties and you feel any unusual bumps, you should get checked out for testicular cancer. Fortunately, it's not a very common cancer in any age group. The second possibility is a condition called torsion, in which the tube attached to the testicle twists, cutting off its blood supply. This condition can be serious, and would probably be causing you serious pain. The third usual cause of sore testicles is an infection, which could require treatment with some kind of antibiotics. Whether the cause of your pain is one of these three or something entirely different, the first step is the same: any time you have bleeding, pain, or any kind of noticeable change in a body part, you should see your doctor for an immediate expert opinion.

Q **Someone told me there is a connection between the size of your nose and the size of your penis. Are they just pulling my leg?**

A They may be pulling your leg, but to answer your question, the alleged connection is just another sexual myth. This one probably got started when someone noticed that the penis and the nose are the only non-bony body parts that protrude from the midline of the human body. Interestingly enough, there is a similarity between the nose and penis that has nothing to do with relative size. In most people, the lining of the nose swells during sexual arousal, just like the penis and clitoris. This is because the lining of the nose is also composed of erectile tissue. To the main question, though, the answer is still no. There is no ratio that describes the size of a man's penis based on the size of his nose, or on the size of his hands or ego, either.

Q **My penis seems to get erect whenever it feels like it, sometimes at very embarrassing moments. I don't always want to pitch a tent in mixed company. What am I supposed to do?**

A All erections are involuntary. They can arise from sexual arousal, climbing a tree, thinking about a favorite piece of music, or remembering a great date. And in the lives of all men, sooner or later, they happen at what seems to be the worst possible moment.

Preventing this is impossible, but you can deal with the situation as it comes up. If you are seated, remain in your chair. If you must get up, hold something in front of you, or, before standing, try to think of the least sexy thing you can: baseball statistics, how the raccoon looked after you ran it over on the freeway, your Aunt Brunhilde, whatever.

I guess the most important thing to remember, guys, is that you really don't have any control over where or when your little private comes to attention. This is why adolescent girls spend so much time giggling, pointing, and generally embarrassing adolescent boys. Since most female plumbing is indoor, when a girl gets excited, it's inconspicuous. As for you guys who think you're the boss of your erection crew, most men have several inadvertent ones throughout the night without ever realizing it, because they're asleep.

Q **I'm a guy, and sometimes I find it hard to urinate in a public washroom. Do I have a problem?**

A The inability to use a public urinal is sometimes known as stage fright, and you can probably already guess why. It's nothing to worry about, and if you find the problem too uncomfortable, you can always just duck into a stall. You'll probably find you'll have no trouble urinating once you have the privacy of a wall, two dividers, and a door surrounding you.

Q **I've heard that circumcised men have more sensitive penises than uncircumcised men. Any truth to the story?**

A No truth at all. Penis sensitivity and male sexual problems have nothing to do with whether a man has a foreskin attached to him or not. Sex therapists will tell you that the men they see with erection, ejaculation, or sensory difficulties are not predominantly circumcised or non-circumcised.

I've never understood why I was circumcised. I feel it is an immoral practice that should be made illegal, and that most women prefer uncircumcised males. How can I have my foreskin restored?

(1) They say parents who circumcise their sons are the most optimistic people in the world: before they know how long it's going to be, they cut some of it off. The decision to cut, or not to cut, is made by parents when their baby boy is...well, a baby. At that point, you were still five years away from making a wild guess at an informed decision, and probably at least five months away from your first word ("da-da," most likely). So your folks decided. (2) As to the morality of the decision, in many cases the choice is made on a religious or cultural basis. It's a debate that is centuries old, and certainly won't be settled by me. (3) Interestingly enough, while the arguments have raged through the eons on the ethics of circumcision, they have also swung like a pendulum in the medical world. For decades in North America, it was thought that circumcision was a healthy practice that would prevent infections and disease. Later, that idea was debunked and doctors began advising their patients against circumcising their infant sons. Now it seems the medical popularity of the little snip is again on the rise, fueled in part by a resurgence in some problems associated with keeping the foreskin intact. (4) Only one medical fact is well documented, and it is this: cancer of the penis, while admittedly rare, has *never* been diagnosed in a circumcised man. (5) Current research (some people will study anything) shows that many women prefer circumcised men.

Besides surgery, there are those who advocate exercises to regrow the foreskin, including stretching the skin that still exists with rubber bands, or hanging weights from the penis. It seems to me these practices are a classic case of investing far too much for a very small return. Mostly, you find advocates of these techniques in support groups for those who think their parents ruined their sex lives. My guess is that the men in these groups are angry at their parents for much more than this, and that their circumcision is just the tip of the problem.

 My partner sometimes takes up to an hour to ejaculate. Is there something I can do to help him?

An hour is a very long time, and while some people think you can never have too much of a good thing, the truth is often the reverse when it comes to sex. After extended periods of time, your genitals can go numb, fall asleep, or just not have as good a time as they might, had the adventure been a little shorter in duration. Some guys have difficulty reaching orgasm because they are too concerned with their partner having one. This is called a retarded ejaculation, as opposed to a premature ejaculation, though I really don't like either term.

Your first step is to ask him if he might not be trying for a world record in order to enhance *your* pleasure, in which case you can let him know that enough is enough. If that's not the case, encourage him to get a full physical to rule out biological causes, such as circulatory problems.

I've always wondered: how fast does a man ejaculate?

Ejaculate leaves a man's body at 45 km/h (28 mph), and no, I don't know what brand of radar gun was used to get these results. If you mean the time elapsed from the first moment he thinks about sex to the moment it actually happens, your guess is as good as mine. The possibilities range from a couple of minutes to a couple of hours. Why, were you thinking of going for the record?

I'm fifty, and rapidly losing my ability to have a firm erection. I can get one, but the engorged blood vessels don't seem to trap the blood long enough for self-pleasure or intercourse. I asked my doctor to send me to a urologist, but he didn't think it was necessary, so here I sit, limp and frustrated.

It's unfortunate that your doctor doesn't think you have a problem — obviously *his* equipment is working just fine. My guess is that if his was lying around snoozing in his lap, he'd be rushing to consult with some of his colleagues.

Remember that your doctor is not your mummy or daddy: you don't have to take his no for an answer. Many causes of erection difficulty can be remedied with exercise or medical intervention. I would suggest you ask for a second opinion, preferably from a urologist, and if your family doctor is unwilling to do that, perhaps you should look for a new family doctor. Remember that they are service providers, not gods, and it is your body they're servicing.

Could you please tell me what it means if a forty-one-year-old man climaxes without any contact whatsoever, before our foreplay even gets started? Is this premature ejaculation? Is he just really turned on? Is he just oversexed? Is this a common problem? And, finally, is it common for men to be able to climax five to six times in one night?

A It seems to me that if you have a forty-one-year-old man who can reach orgasm six times in one night, you aren't complaining, you're bragging. Unless he's wearing you out, I don't think you have much to worry about. First of all, the penis is not a snow tire — you can't wear it out from overuse. Just about any man can have several orgasms, though probably not without at least some rest in between (it's called the refractory period). If a man reaches orgasm before foreplay and that's it for the night, you might be talking about premature ejaculation. If a man reaches orgasm before foreplay and then has a few more during the main event and beyond, then you're probably just turning him on like crazy. It sounds like your guy just finds you incredibly attractive. Do you still think you have a problem?

Q **I have tiny bumps all over my genitals. They are quite itchy and irritate me at night. What do I have, and what can I do to cure it?**

A The first thing you should do is take your body to your doctor. Your itchy bumps could be anything from pubic lice, herpes, or genital warts to a plain old everyday skin rash, and your family physician gets paid to determine which possibility is the reality. Your skin is the largest organ of your body, and anything that affects or infects the skin can affect or infect it anywhere, including your pubic area. It may be nothing, or it may be everything, and the longer you wait to see your doctor, the longer you may be worrying too much about little, or too little about much.

Q **My husband wakes up every morning with an erection. He says it's because I'm so attractive — I say he just has to go to the bathroom. Who's right?**

A Actually, neither of you is right. In fact, your husband probably has regular erections through the night while he sleeps. On average, a man has five or six per night, with the last coming in the morning just before he wakes up. That's why it's there to greet you first thing each morning. Researchers believe the overnight erections are part of the body's way of checking and maintaining blood flow to the extremities, sort of a test cycle. Of course, the fact that an erection arrives on its own in no way prevents most guys from wanting to put it to a wholly voluntary purpose.

Q **Masturbating has lost its fun for me — just wham, bam, wash your hand. Could you give me some tips to make things more interesting again?**

A My suggestion is to give it a rest! I think your body is probably trying to tell you something. If masturbation has lost its appeal, maybe you should try spending your time in other pursuits, like constructing a bird bath, doing the laundry, taking up bonsai gardening — whatever. I hope you're not holding yourself to some kind of schedule in which you must have so many orgasms per week to prove you're a real human being. There's more to life than sex, and the sound of one hand clapping is not applause.

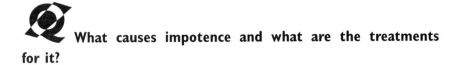 **My boyfriend of four years cannot seem to maintain an erection when he decides to have sex with me. We attempt it about once every three weeks and I'm starting to feel it's me physically. If I was really sexy, wouldn't I turn him on? I've tried talking with him but we can't figure it out. He is also very conservative so trying interesting things is out.**

Rest assured it is not your attractiveness that is responsible for his ordeal. You're in a bit of a bind: it won't work and he won't try anything new.

First of all, about the erection itself. Just because he decides at a certain time to have sex with you does not mean he's turned on. That has nothing to do with you — it has to do with him being in tune with his body and his emotions. A lot of guys figure their little soldier should be at their beck and call, ready and able to do whatever they tell it, regardless of how the rest of their body and mind happens to be feeling at the time.

He's very conservative, he decides what you can do, what you can't do, and when you can have sex. I'd suggest you take less responsibility for what's going on here, back off from the issue of sex itself, and see whether in fact this relationship has some dents or cracks in other places. My guess is the problem isn't merely centered on sexuality.

What causes impotence and what are the treatments for it?

There are many causes, ranging from the psychological to the medical. In the former category, consider that you may not be really interested in your current partner. If it wilts, your lower body may be trying to send your brain a message. You also have to consider how you feel about the idea of sex in general. Do you think it's a healthy part of living? Or something dirty, deserving punishment? There are other, more organic causes, including blood supply problems to that unit, or damage to nerves controlling erection.

Treatment depends on whether it is primary impotence or secondary. Primary impotence involves either psychological causes or physical problems with the male unit itself. The secondary type involves impotence caused as a side effect of some drug or from some other injury to the body. Psychologically induced impotence is best handled in a counseling situation. Where the root is physical, and the original cause can't be eliminated, impotence can be treated with either medication or prosthetic implants designed to create a pseudo-erection. Among the drugs in use for this problem are an injection used for paraplegics who want to be able to have a family, and a testosterone patch for men whose problem can be traced to a deficiency in that hormone.

I've been dating a man for three and a half years and our sex life is dead. His sex drive is so low, he can't even maintain an erection lately, and we have sex barely once a month. I've always been a very sexual person and since we began seeing each other, I've had to sacrifice a lot. I love him, and the rest of our relationship is great, but can we survive together if our sex drives are so far out of sync?

Although you are probably looking for sexual causes to this problem, it's very possible his lack of erection stems from other things in his life — stress, worry, or sickness. It sounds like there's something going on he's not telling you about. Ask him, and hopefully you'll get an honest reply.

Sex drives come and go even in people who are extremely active sexually. It's not unusual for people to have droughts in the middle of an otherwise overflowing sex life. If we rule out the possibility that he's suffering from poor nutrition or some other medical condition, and assuming he isn't on some new medication with side effects in that area, then the idea of something psychological going on becomes more probable. In that case, you should talk with him about it.

Unfortunately for most men, anxiety-induced erection problems tend to multiply. If his erection disappears once and he worries about that, then the next time he'll focus his attention on whether it will happen again, so of course it does. Soon enough, he has a whole case history of erection problems, and then he starts expecting it to happen: his worry brings about his worst fantasy. Sometimes the best way to deal with an erection problem is to back away from it. One thing is certain: yelling at it will not make it stand at attention.

Q I've been with my boyfriend for almost two years now, and we're living together. We had a so-so sex life at first, but now he's not interested in having sex at all. Last night he told me he wants us to get married some day, but how will my sex life be then? Please help me!

A Your first step should probably be to rule out any possible medical problem. A checkup at the family M.D. is the only way to make sure his moving parts are in proper order, and to rule out illnesses and conditions that can detract from sexual interest.

Once you're sure his unit isn't on the fritz, you can consider that many people find sexual frequency diminishing after the heat of a new relationship starts to cool off. You might want to have a conversation with him about what he needs to get the party going. His requirements may be reasonably easy to arrange, and enjoyable as a bonus. The other possibility is that he is just one of those men who have a low sex drive. One thing is probable: if there's very little sex going on now, your situation is unlikely to be altered merely by a change in marital status.

Q My boyfriend and I have oral sex quite often, so I'm curious about the contents of semen. Is it fattening? Is it nutritious? Can it contribute to tooth decay?

A Healthy semen consists of about thirty ingredients, ranging from fructose and Vitamin C to lactic acid and various salts and enzymes — in other words, sugar and spice and everything nice. There's really not enough of it in the average 10-milliliter ejaculation to be fattening, and it doesn't cause cavities either, though brushing your teeth afterward is probably still a good idea. It also won't clear up your complexion, grow hair on your face, or lower your voice. About the only thing healthy sperm will do is cause babies, though not through oral sex.

Q My husband takes a shower every morning, but by the time evening rolls around, he gets a little smelly. I happen to like his smell, and he thinks I'm weird for it. Is he right?

A Absolutely not. The smell is the result of pheromones, and while the actual odor can be stronger or weaker in different people, there are some researchers who believe they are the reason people are attracted to each other in the first place. The entire perfume industry was built around the idea of odor creating attraction between people, so it should come as no surprise that some people have sensitive enough noses to pick up natural body smells that they enjoy.

A guy I know was recently diagnosed with cancer of the testicles. By the time he went to the doctor, the original tumor was the size of a softball and the cancer had spread across his body. How could he have walked around with a swollen testicle for a year without noticing that something was wrong?

In recent years, women have been scared into thinking that whether they think it's necessary or not, they should check their breasts for lumps monthly. Every woman knows this part of her anatomy has the potential to be the recipient of bad things, and should be attended to. Unfortunately, because men don't go through monthly cycles, few realize their testicles need to be checked out on a regular basis. In fact, men should probably do a monthly check in the shower to make sure their testicles are smooth to the touch, just as women do their monthly breast self-examination. Any thickening or lumps felt in a testicle should be brought to the attention of your doctor.

Testicular cancer primarily strikes men in their early twenties or even younger. Ironically, this is the time in a man's life when he is least likely to imagine that anything could need attention, and so he is least likely to be watching for it.

I'm seventeen and I want to get my penis pierced. My dad hit the roof when I told him, and said "No way," to be polite about it. I think he's being unreasonable — after all, it's my body, not his. What do you think?

A Sorry, but I think the reasoning difficulty lies with you. No seventeen-year-old should be putting holes in a body part to which he has barely been introduced.

Your penis is a very delicate instrument, fueled by a blood supply running through tiny little vessels and various spongy tissues, which in turn feed even tinier cells. Added to this most important function is the fact that the blood traveling in and out is also what makes it erect or relaxed. If anything goes wrong while you are poking holes in it, you could be faced with a lifetime of impotence — a rather large price to risk paying for a new place to hang a bangle, don't you think?

Maybe by the time you're twenty-five or thirty, you'll be ready to take this kind of gamble, but seventeen? I think not. In ten or twelve years, perhaps you'll have seen it all, done it all, and be ready to take the chance that it will hang limp for the rest of your years. In the meantime, maybe you can try piercing your ears first, and if you really love that, go on to your nose and lips. With three or four holes in your head already, you may be satisfied without moving lower in your anatomy.

Q My boyfriend says if he doesn't have enough sex, the pressure in his testicles builds up and he ends up with excruciating pain. He says there's even a medical name for his condition — "blue balls." I say he's just horny. Who's right?

A There is a condition sometimes called "blue balls," known to the medical community as vasocongestion of the testicles. It's like a lot of people getting ready for a party and then not being able to go, so they just stand around, bump into one another, and feel crowded. This does not, however, mean that you have to be the chauffeur to take the gang to the big event. Your boyfriend can certainly take care of this problem himself when it arises — by being his own driver, if you catch my drift.

Keep in mind that this is one of the oldest ploys men have used to obtain a sex partner: he'll just die in agony if he doesn't get some, and you're the one to give it to him. There is no doubt that it may be serious enough to cause a lot of pain and discomfort, but it's a condition that can easily be relieved by the person who has the problem.

I'm a very hairy guy, and while I'm very self-conscious about it, I'd never think of shaving my body. Please give me a woman's point of view on this problem. Should I just stay with the collared shirts and long pants, or do I need to develop a new Hair Pride routine?

When it comes to bodies, there are some adjustments people can make. With hair, you can shave or wax or use electrolysis, but it seems like an awful lot of energy for such a small return. Lots of women don't care about how hairy or smooth you are, and some even get turned on by the idea of a really hairy guy. As for the few women who would avoid dating you for this one reason, the pool of possibilities only diminishes minimally. There are still millions of women available. Wear whatever clothes you like. Suit yourself.

The other day, while having sex, I was on top and I leaned backward, perhaps too far. My boyfriend yelled and pushed me off him. Two days later, his penis was still hurting him. Could he have some serious injury?

A It is actually possible to "sprain" or "break" a penis. It's an injury that usually occurs when an abrupt change of direction takes place, and the penis, as flexible as it may be, is unable to negotiate the move. If your boyfriend's penis is still hurting two days later, he should certainly take it to the doctor to be checked out.

Q **Aside from falling on the bar of a bicycle, are there any common ways a penis can be injured?**

A Yes, there are. In fact, a bicycle can cause an injury even without your falling onto the bar between your legs. If your seat is not adjusted properly, you can numb the nerve that runs along the base of your penis, a condition called penile anesthesia — a literal numbing of the unit. Fortunately, this problem is temporary, and easily prevented by pointing the horn of your bike seat downward.

It's also possible to get frostbite down there if you head out into the winter cold without properly insulated clothing. This is treated medically in the same way a frostbitten nose or hand or toe would be.

The penis can be injured, sometimes severely, by bending it too far down when erect. If your partner is on top when you have sex, be careful she doesn't lean too far over in the throes of passion.

Other problems include foreign objects being introduced into the penis ("Mr. Happy, meet Mr. Crochet Hook"), either intentionally or inadvertently, and of course, getting caught on the zipper when closing or opening your pants. No doubt these injuries all sound uncomfortable at best and downright painful at worst — and they are. Always treat your big boy with the care and respect it deserves.

11

The Female Unit

The woman is constructed in such a way that she could probably go her whole life without even knowing she has genitals. When she looks down, she sees her toes, unlike a man, who looks down and sees his equipment dangling in front of him (see Chapter 10, "The Male Unit"). As a result, a woman needs to send out a search party to discover both what she has and what it looks like — from her perspective, she can never really eyeball it without a series of mirrors or a remote-control video camera. The only other option is to consult a textbook on the female unit, which will show her equipment, albeit splayed across the pages like some bizarre old-fashioned butterfly collection.

Unfortunately, none of these alternatives gives a woman much of a sense of what's going on down there, and added to the mystery is the fact that the parts that give her pleasure are so much smaller than those on a man. Dr. Lonnie Barbach describes women's genitals as like a pair of socks — all neatly folded up and tucked away in the drawer. If you want to really examine them, you have to poke around in the dark.

Is it true that hickeys can cause cancer when given on the breasts? And is there an easy way to get rid of them?

A hickey brings blood to the surface of the skin by applying negative pressure to the outside of the skin. A hickey is, to put it simply, a bruise. It's more unsightly than dangerous, and probably explains the invention of the turtleneck sweater.

Just like other bruises, hickeys will fade in a few days, but if you need to cover one up sooner (like for a job interview), folk cures range from rubbing toothpaste or alcohol on it, to pressing a cold fork against it. The only reliable method I know of is the thick cover stick you can get at your favorite makeup department.

I'm sixteen, and my boyfriend and I are planning to sleep together. The first time a woman has sex, does she bleed a lot?

Not necessarily. Some women are born with a hymen, some without. Some hymens have more perforations than others, but all have some kind of tear, rip, or hole — if they didn't, virgins wouldn't be able to have their periods, or use tampons.

There is no sure-fire test for virginity, and throughout history, those who thought differently were only fooling themselves. There was a time in Europe when it was common practice to hang the bloodstained bed sheets out in plain view on the morning after the wedding night. This was presumably to prove that the marriage was consummated, and that the bride was a virgin. A closer inspection of those bed sheets would probably have found that, more often than not, the blood belonged to last night's beef dinner, not yesterday's virgin.

Q I consider myself a fairly normal twenty-five-year-old woman, but I've never had an orgasm, and I know at least two other women who haven't either. Is this normal, are we doing something wrong, or is it our choice of partners?

A Odd as this may sound, it has nothing to do with your partners, and everything to do with you. After all, it is *your* orgasm we're talking about — or your lack of one, to be precise. Getting a different boyfriend is not going to get you past your impasse.

Barring medical problems, nearly all women are capable of having orgasms. For some, however, it certainly takes more work and practice to have one than it does for a man. Part of it has to do with the concealed location of a woman's equipment. Probably the best place to start is with yourself, alone. Masturbation may be one of your taboos, but how are you going to tell your partner exactly what feels good to you if you don't know yourself?

Q When I masturbate and have an orgasm, my feet cramp and sometimes hurt so much I can hardly walk for a few minutes afterward. Is this normal?

A Some women can actually get orgasms by tensing their muscles. In fact, in some old Japanese prints, a sign of orgasm is when women are depicted with their toes curled.

My first guess on your problem is that you are unknowingly tensing your lower leg and foot muscles when climaxing, leading to your cramping problem. If your only problem is being unable to walk for a few minutes after having an orgasm, my question is, what's the rush? Relax and bathe in the afterglow before you go for that jog to wherever. If your discomfort level is greater than that, a doctor or physiotherapist can probably recommend exercises to keep the cramps from happening in the first place.

 About Pap smears — what exactly are they?

A First, your gynecologist or family doctor will insert a speculum, which parts the walls of your vagina to allow a clear view. This may be uncomfortable but should not be painful, and yes, it is necessary — until *something* is inserted, the walls of the vagina remain closed against each other. Your doctor will then take a swab of cells from your cervix (the "smear" in "Pap smear") and send them off to the lab for analysis. The screeners look for abnormal cells, and the amount they find determines the number they assign to the result. Pap test results range from 1 to 5, and while 1 may be best, you shouldn't panic if your doctor says the result was a 2.

Your cervix is basically a ring forming the boundary between two different kinds of body tissue. Your uterus is on one side, your vagina is on the other, and the two parts are made up of different kinds of cells. Acting as the mediator between these different kinds of tissues, the cells of the cervix can sometimes become "confused" — that's why it's not unusual for a woman's test results to go from a 1 to a 3, before sliding back down the scale to 1 again. It doesn't mean you had cancer (indicated by a 5), it just means some of your cervical cells took on the aspects of the cells on either side.

 When are you supposed to start getting Pap smears?

 The Pap test should be part of your regular, yearly gynecological examination, beginning either when you turn eighteen or when you become sexually active, whichever comes first. Please don't schedule your appointment when you have your period, or if you have vaginitis or an STD — all of these will skew the results.

 Do I really have to get Pap smears?

 Yes. You do.

 Why does the vagina grow bigger during sex?

 For openers, the vagina is not really an organ in and of itself — it's a potential space. Before arousal, like the bellows of an accordion, the walls are collapsed against each other. During arousal, or delivery of a baby, the boundaries of your vagina move apart, far enough to accommodate anything from the size of a finger to a small turkey. It may be just a space, but it's a very versatile space indeed.

I really enjoy having my breasts sucked and fondled during sex, but someone recently told me too much stimulation can cause breast cancer later. Is this true?

There is no indication that cancer can be caused by having one's breasts overstimulated, during sex or otherwise. The whole idea makes no sense, especially when you consider that a baby spends a lot more time at the breast in one year than the average man does in a lifetime. It makes even less sense when you consider that some research suggests that breastfeeding actually helps *prevent* cancer.

The causes of breast cancer are still not entirely clear, but there seems to be a genetic link. Factors influencing your likelihood of getting it appear to include family history of the disease, early menstruation, late menopause, a lack of children, or having your first child after age thirty. Even if your life fits most items on this list, however, it still does not mean you will definitely get breast cancer. Your best course of prevention is monthly self-examinations, regular checkups with your doctor, and an immediate visit to your physician if you do notice any lumps or other changes in your breast tissue.

My girlfriend likes to have sex during her period. I find it gross. How are we going to deal with this?

A Turn out the lights. Then it will all be just wet girl stuff, and you won't know the difference. Also, do it on a towel, and keep a washcloth handy. Often the flow will stop during sexual intercourse. If not, some women use a diaphragm to temporarily stop the flow. Either way, a bath afterward will take care of anything that seeps through.

If you're still turned off, your simplest option is to avoid having sex during the five days or so that it takes for most women to complete their monthly period. Keep in mind, however, that your girlfriend is not alone: many women are more aroused in the time around their period. This may be because of internal stimulus from the blood in the pelvic area, or the hormonal changes a woman goes through just before her period. If you still don't want to have a complete sexual experience at that time of the month, remember that there are many other types of sex beyond actual intercourse.

Q Settle an argument for me — which are more sensitive, small breasts or large?

A In this competition, the tiny ones have it! The reason is simple: all breasts have the same number of nerve endings, whether they fit in a triple-D-cup bra, or a single-A.

Imagine that nerve endings are silver dollars, small breasts are baseballs, and large breasts are basketballs. You have three silver dollars to paste at equal distances apart on a baseball, and three more to paste at equal distances apart on a basketball. Now imagine being able to keep as many silver dollars as you can touch, with one hand, at the same time. Gripping the baseball firmly, it's easy for even a small hand to touch all three silver dollars. But on the basketball, you'll only get one, and that's if you aim your grip properly. All of this means that per square inch, a small breast feels more than a large one, and so does the woman attached to it.

The only note to be added here is that there are also individual differences in how much of an erogenous zone the breast is in the first place. That means there's always going to be a woman out there with huge gazongas that are more sensitive than another woman with little peaches. They are the exceptions.

Who named the clitoris, and for that matter, how do you pronounce "clitoris"?

You say "cli-TOR-is," and I say "CLI-tor-is." Perhaps the more important question is not who named it, but why. The truth is that no one really wants to say the word out loud because it was designed to make you feel silly or embarrassed when you do. It was obviously named by someone who didn't want anyone talking about it.

This logic also holds true for the other body parts located in your lower midsection. Look at how the rest of your body is named: nice, simple, easy-to-remember, one-syllable words like *nose, ear, arm, leg, toe. Finger* is about as complicated as it gets. Let your gaze wander down to what are commonly called the "private" parts, and suddenly Latin isn't so dead a language any more: *penis, vagina, clitoris, vas deferens, mons pubis, labia majora* and *minora, uterus.*

Body parts with any sexual meaning all seem to have been named by someone who wanted to establish some distance between himself and his body (safe to say it was probably *not* a woman). He wanted to establish that distance in the worst way, and so he did. Of course, none of that explains why we are still stuck with the terminology. It does, however, go a long way toward explaining why your private parts have so many more slang names than your public parts.

Q **What's the story on breast reduction surgery? I thought you could only have the operation once, but a friend of mine says she had it done again after a pregnancy pumped her back up to double-D cups.**

A Doctors prefer that you have one reduction and leave it at that, but pregnancy certainly can cause a lasting increase in bust size. For this reason, many doctors will suggest you wait until you've finished having your family before undergoing the reduction.

On the other hand, if you're still in your teenage years and your breasts are already enormous, you may not want to wait a couple of decades to have something done about it. Also, many women who have had the procedure feel incredibly happy about the results, and say they wish they'd done it sooner.

Finally, improvements in medical procedure itself have eliminated some of the negative effects of breast reduction. Women who had the earlier procedures were often left with no sensation in their nipples. The newer surgery has cured that problem by changing the way the doctor makes incisions in the breasts.

Q **I'm sixteen and my breasts haven't even started growing yet. I've read that if one doesn't show much development by this age, medical attention is required. Is this true?**

A The bodies of most girls attain the proportions of an adult woman somewhere between the ages of twelve and nineteen. Most girls show at least some increase in size by age fifteen, though their pubic hair may still be quite sparse. If you're sixteen and your breasts have not begun to change in any way at all, first ask your mother when she started developing — sometimes late bloomers run in families. Then, you're probably best off to see your doctor. All the modifications that take place as a girl becomes a woman are dependent upon hormonal and chemical changes in her body, and your doctor can check to see if those metabolic alterations are taking place. It's possible you might need some kind of treatment to help them along.

My girlfriend insists there are two types of female orgasms, clitoral and vaginal. I say all orgasms are the same. Who's right?

The vaginal orgasm is a myth that dates back to Freud. We all start out in the womb with the same genital bud. Sometime in the nine months before birth, the bud develops into either a clitoris or a penis. Both have exactly the same number of nerve endings, and both are the root of the orgasm (so to speak). The feelings of orgasm may spread to other parts of the body, but they all start in the same two places: the penis for men, the clitoris for women.

Finally, here's one more point of gender convergence for your trivia scorecard. In both the male and female orgasms, the genital muscles contract rhythmically every four-fifths of a second. Those muscles do not indicate the *site* of the orgasm, they merely mark the fact that an orgasm is taking place. Women may feel their orgasms in different parts of their bodies on different occasions, which probably goes a long way toward explaining the staying power of this particular myth. Still, you may rest assured: all female orgasms may not be created equal, but they are all created in the same place.

Q **I really like my body except for my breasts. Or should I say, lack of breasts. I really wish they were bigger. Are there any non-surgical remedies?**

A Yes, there are — getting pregnant and, for some, taking birth-control pills. It should be noted that both are temporary fixes and rather radical measures to avail oneself of an extra inch. Instead, why not try changing your thought process, and making friends with your boobies. The majority of men surveyed say they don't much care about the size of your chest accessories, and there are vast advantages to having a sleeker topside (take it from me, I know): (1) When you jog, you will not flog yourself to death. (2) When you're older, you won't be playing soccer with them. (3) Bras are optional. There are many more, but I think you get the points without my enlarging on them.

Q **My problem is my behind — it's too large. My friends all say I'm being ridiculous, I know I'm attractive, I think I have a pretty nice shape... It's just that when I'm trying on clothes in a store and look at myself in a mirror, I still can't help wishing it was smaller. Is there any way to spot-reduce that part of my body, or any way I can hide it altogether?**

A Your friends are probably right when they say you look just fine. After all, when a whole gaggle of people are of one opinion, they're often correct. Also, one of the advantages of that body part is that it's behind you. It's hard to see and easy to forget about — if you put your mind to it.

The first thing you can do is stop looking at yourself in three-way store mirrors. Consider that when you sit down, you have a nice soft cushion, where others have uncomfortable bony rears. Exercise is never a bad thing, but how much it will help will depend on your body shape, and your current fitness level. As for camouflage, dark colors will make you look smaller to a point, but it's still how you look at it that's important, or how you *don't* look at it.

Seven months ago, my husband and I had our first baby. We've resumed our sex life, which is going relatively well except for one problem — my breasts. Though my husband doesn't agree it's a problem (thank goodness), I am literally turned off by the sight of them. I know I'm being shallow about this. Can you give me some advice on how to deal with it?

Pregnancy creates a hormonal change in women that lessens the density of breast tissue. It happens to every mother to a greater or lesser degree, so there's really not much you can do to reverse the changes. Working out with weights will help strengthen the muscles behind your breasts, but the simplest solution is to find a new bra you think is attractive, and learn to make friends with your new chest accessories. Your husband still thinks you look great. You thought enough of his taste to marry him in the first place, so why not just assume that he's right? You do look great.

My boyfriend put the tip of his penis inside me, but it only went in about an inch. Am I still a virgin?

A A virgin is a person who has not had sexual intercourse. One inch would qualify as at least a starting attempt, so technically, you're probably no longer a virgin. However, a lot of these things are negotiable, so if you still *feel* like a virgin, who's to say you can't still call yourself one? There are no virgin police out there peeking through keyholes and writing down names, and no one is going to decide you were lying and haul you off to court for non-virginity.

Consider also the difference between a virgin and a sexually innocent or inexperienced person. There are people who have done everything — and I do mean *everything* — except have intercourse. Technically, those people are virgins. On the other hand, there are non-virgins whose only sexual experience was just that: intercourse, once. Technical definitions aside, who is more the virgin here? I say if you want to be a virgin, you are.

Q **Why do female nipples come in so many different sizes and shapes?**

A Probably for the same reason female breasts come in all shapes and sizes. In fact, females in general come in all shapes and sizes. Variety is the spice of life, haven't you heard? Nipple variations occur regardless of breast variation, not in proportion to them, and in fact, there is no mathematical relationship between the size of nipples and any other part of the body. There is also no relationship between penis and hand size, or penis and nose size (more urban myths).

To my knowledge, there is only one odd ratio in the human body that holds true for the majority of people on the planet: the distance between your outstretched hands, fingertips to fingertips, is equal to your height. It's the basis of a famous diagram drawn by Leonardo da Vinci. If you don't believe me, get out a tape measure and try it.

So, back to nipples and breasts. Why so many sizes? I say it's just one of nature's many variations on a theme, designed by evolution so that we don't get bored staring at the same body on everyone.

Q **My girlfriend has a pungent fragrance down there, and it makes oral sex a lot less than fun. I'm too embarrassed to tell her, but now I'm avoiding oral sex. Any suggestions?**

A Other than a snorkel and mask — which she'd probably notice even in the dark — the barrier method probably won't work. If you're intimate enough to have sex, you're intimate enough to talk about sex, and about things putting your sex life on hold. Your girlfriend could have a medical problem that needs attending, so dive right in and tell her. But gently. And not while you're actually having sex, okay?

Q **I've been on birth-control pills for the last eight years, but now my husband and I want to start a family, so I'm going off them. My question is, do I have to wait a while before trying to have a baby, or should we go ahead now?**

A I know of no medical reason why you can't start shooting for parenthood as soon as you read this. Taking birth-control pills merely fakes your body into believing you're pregnant. Therefore, ovulation does not occur. When you stop taking the pill, your body starts ovulating again. This may take one month or several months, but regardless, the hormones in the pill should not affect an embryo. Don't be surprised if it takes you six months or longer to get pregnant, though. Many women stop taking the pill and are amazed they don't get pregnant within twenty-four hours. And remember that building your baby should still be fun.

 How do you tell when a woman is faking her orgasm?

You might as well ask how they get the Caramilk in the Caramilk bar. You can stay up all night with a flashlight and a magnifying glass if you like — unless you have access to the testing equipment at the Kinsey Institute, and a partner willing to let you attach it to her, you aren't ever going to be able to tell. There are, however, some signs most women exhibit when an orgasm does occur. Most women get erect nipples when they arrive, and the muscles of their vaginas will contract rhythmically, every four-fifths of a second. (I don't suggest you keep a stopwatch handy for timing them.)

Ironically, fake orgasms often backfire on the woman involved. *She* is trying to keep *him* from feeling inadequate. Unfortunately, this means the poor guy will then try to remember every single move, since it apparently brought about such intense pleasure, and will only succeed in evoking another great acting performance next time around. I bring all this up as a preamble to this important message to all women: *stop* faking it.

When my boyfriend and I are making love, as much as I enjoy it, sometimes when he penetrates, it really hurts. I'm really aroused, so that's not the problem, and it seems to happen just some of the time. Is there anything I can do to prevent this?

A You may find that a change of position helps. Although there aren't a lot of nerve endings in the back two-thirds of the vagina, some women find getting their cervix bumped about during sex can be uncomfortable. You might want to change to a position in which you have more control of the action — something other than the missionary position. Try getting on top or making love on the side, so you can control how much of your partner is inside you. Whether that approach works or not, you should probably also check with your doctor, just to make sure you don't have an infection or other medical problem that needs attention.

Q **When I have sex with my girlfriend near the time of her period, she experiences sharp pains in her abdomen. Sometimes she even becomes nauseated. Is this normal?**

A Well, not if she likes you. The pain she's experiencing probably has to do with the changes in hormone levels that a women goes through around the time of her period. It could also be something she should look into medically, such as endometriosis. Whichever answer applies to your girlfriend, no regular, internal body discomfort should be ignored — unless of course it's just you that makes her sick. In that case, a relationship change may be just the cure for who ails her.

Q **I really enjoy having sex, but some of the time when I don't have an orgasm, I feel uncomfortable, or even sore. What's going on?**

A Sometimes if there has been a buildup of sexual excitement with no resolution, women can get pelvic congestion. Think of it as getting a traffic jam in your lower midsection. The condition can often can be relieved simply by having an orgasm on your own. Next time it happens, the helping hand you need could be your own.

Q My new boyfriend is so large he frightens me. What would happen if you had sex with a really large man?

A For the most part, when it comes to sex, the human race is one-size-fits-all. You should remember that this part of your body is designed as a baby's entrance to the world, so unless we're talking about a guy who's bigger than a champagne bottle or a medium-sized chicken, there should be a way for your two ends to meet. Arousal, lubrication, and desire should take care of it. Many overly endowed men have told me they find technique to be the most important thing for them — not rushing things and letting their partner get used to how big they really are. The final word here is that the human body is built from a truly wonderful design: when it comes to coming together, where there's a will, there's almost always a way.

Q My new partner is a twenty-five-year-old virgin who has strong pain associated with inserting a finger into her vagina, so we do not attempt intercourse. Although she would like to share this intimacy with me, I do not want to physically hurt her in the process. Is there something we can do to ease her great vaginal discomfort?

First of all, despite her assurances, you have to be certain your partner really is ready and willing to have intercourse. There is a condition called vaginismus that results in a painful spasm of the vagina, a condition most often associated with emotional conflict. The intense contraction of the muscles surrounding the vagina makes intercourse painful or impossible. If this is your partner's problem, she may have moral, ethical, religious, or emotional barriers to sex, despite what she says to the contrary. Counseling may help sort out the barriers in her head, and a registered sex therapist or physician can help with the mechanics of the problem. First and foremost, however, she should see her doctor and rule out any medical problem that may be in play.

After three years with my boyfriend, I've only had one orgasm with him during sex. When I'm by myself, I seem to have no problem, but if he's there, even masturbation is a failure. I'm exasperated, he's frustrated, and no matter how many positions or techniques we try, it's still no-go. What should I do?

Only 30 percent of women have orgasms solely through intercourse. The other 70 percent also require manual, oral, or other kinds of stimulation in order to come — it's entirely possible you're just one of the vast majority. As one expert puts it, the "Look Ma no hands" orgasm is an unrealistic expectation.

The other thing to consider is that you and your boyfriend are exasperated and frustrated, which makes it sound like you've made your orgasm into some kind of achievement award. The prerequisite for an orgasm is being relaxed enough to have one. If you're exasperated, frustrated, tense, and sitting there with a mental stopwatch ticking away in your head, then no matter what you do, or how many techniques you employ, I doubt you're going to make it to the finish line you've set for yourself.

Sex does not necessarily equal intercourse, and intercourse does not necessarily equal orgasm — it's simply not a mathematical progression that holds true in all cases. Why not relax and stop making this your only goal? You'll probably find that it's the pressure you're putting on yourself that's keeping you from enjoying yourself.

My boyfriend can't give me an orgasm, but don't tell me to masturbate — I don't believe in it. What should I do?

You seem to think an orgasm is like some kind of pizza delivered by your boyfriend. It's *your* orgasm — he has to be responsible for his own. If you bought a car, would you only let your boyfriend drive it? Of course not. Well, it's your body, so why do you only let your boyfriend touch it? I'm sorry, but if you don't know how your body works, you can hardly expect your boyfriend to be an expert. For some reason, most people would admit to bank robbery, tax fraud, or lying to their best friend before they'd admit to touching themselves. Be assured that 99 percent of the population have done it, even if a much smaller percentage will own up to it when the survey people arrive on their doorsteps.

When my boyfriend and I sleep together, I always have an orgasm if I do it myself with a vibrator. Sometimes if I'm on top I feel like I could have an orgasm, but I never seem to get there. I'd like to have one with my boyfriend because I think it would leave me more satisfied. Can you tell me some ideas and good positions?

A Your body really doesn't care what kind of stimulation produces an orgasm, whether it's yourself, another person, or a toy. Since you don't seem to have a problem producing an orgasm yourself, you might want to show your boyfriend what you do to bring one on. Then, he can do likewise. As for positions, you've already picked a good one. With you on top, both his hands and yours are free for all kinds of fun things, in addition to the innies and outies already happening. You can try other positions as well, as long as they're enjoyable for both of you, but don't expect to find some magic juxtaposition of limbs that will make the earth move. And don't get so tied up trying to produce the big O that you forget why it is you're going to bed in the first place.

Q Whenever I have sex with my boyfriend of one and a half years, I start to cry hysterically, and I don't like him touching me until I calm down. Do you have any help for me?

A Crying after an orgasm is officially called *coitus tristus*, which is Latin for "sad intercourse." Some people let go with verbal celebration, squawks, yelps, and/or moans and such. For others, it's laughter or tears. It's no wonder an orgasm can evoke such a wide variety of reactions, considering how small our brains are and how much complicated wiring exists inside them. Orgasms can be very emotional and/or spiritual events. However, your not wanting to be touched may be related to another area — intimacy issues. If this concerns you, or just rings a bell, you might want to consider talking things over with a good counselor.

Q I recently saw a story on television about guys taking hormone treatments to grow breasts before their sex-change operations. Can women use the same treatment to grow larger breasts, instead of getting implants?

A The bodies of both women and men contain both male and female hormones — the difference is the ratio between them. Women have more progesterone and estrogen, men have more testosterone. Men undergoing a sex change to female status do indeed take extra female hormones to stimulate breast growth — in effect, they get more of what they don't have much of. Women, on the other hand, already have female hormones in abundance. Adding more might produce bigger breasts, but quite possibly at the expense of medical problems, such as breast or uterine cancer. Too much estrogen is not good for a woman, and no reputable physician would prescribe more for a woman who just wants bigger breasts. Yes, implants are an option, but they involve a surgical procedure and some potential problems. My suggestion is the miracle bra. It produces maximum cleavage at minimum cost, and at minimal risk to your health.

Q I have hair on my breasts. Is this normal? Should I do anything about it? And if so, what?

A Some women have more body hair than others, whether it's arm hair, leg hair, or, yes, breast hair. This may have something to do with the genetic makeup of your family background or ethnic group, or it may just be the way your particular body happens to work. Most of the time, there is nothing to be concerned about. Extreme amounts of hair on a woman's breasts — also known as hirsutism — may be caused by abnormally high levels of hormones like testosterone. If you think your breasts are very hairy, you should check this possibility out with your doctor. If we're just talking about a few stray hairs around the nipples that are bothering you, snip them off with a pair of scissors — carefully!

My girlfriend and I have an active and enjoyable sex life, but the other day she was diagnosed with a urinary tract infection. Can this have something to do with how often we make love?

Urinary tract infections are much more common in women than men. They can appear without warning or a readily identifiable cause. The bacteria may be finding their way into the tract during or after sexual intercourse, but these are not classed as sexually transmitted diseases. The bacteria may have come from the woman's own body, migrating from one orifice to another during sex (or while swimming, or walking, or whatever).

One of the simplest ways to prevent an infection coming about after sex is to simply go to the bathroom afterward. The urine will wash away any bacteria that have started up the tract, and prevent a problem before it can occur. Men often seem to need to urinate after sex — that may be why men have fewer urinary tract infections. The bottom line, as with all medical conditions, is to see your doctor if you don't feel right in any part of your body.

Why is it that sometimes it seems women have horny moods and men are just plain horny?

The human species is the only one on the planet whose females do not have an estrus cycle. This means most female animals are available for sex a few days a year at most. On the other hand, human females are always available for sex, even if we're not always interested in it.

So when *are* women interested? The surveys say that most women are most easily aroused (in other words, horniest) just before they get their period, somewhat less easily during their period, and least likely to get aroused the rest of the month. This probably has to do with the fluctuating hormone levels a woman experiences as she goes through her monthly cycle. Men, on the other hand, don't have much in the way of hormonal changes through the month (certainly no reproductive cycle). As a result, evolution has decreed that the male human is always ready to procreate the species, so he is left with his fantasies and his ever-ready equipment, waiting for the chance to put it into use.

 Why do men have so many names for a woman's breasts?

You mean like boobs, bazooms, bazookas, gazongas, hooters, rockets, knockers, twin peaks, buicks, dairy arrangements, chest accessories, headlights, pillows, himalayas, muffins, and major-league yaboes? I don't know — maybe it's because the breast is one of their very favorite body parts. If there was a body part of the week, the breast would probably be body part of the decade. Men just spend so much time thinking about breasts, they can't help but come up with a wide variety of euphemisms.

Of course, men don't just nickname a woman's body parts — they also have a number of aliases for their own. Most men also seem to have pet names for their penises, like Sam or Fred or Big Boy (for the most optimistic). Why do men name their equipment? A certain cynic once suggested it was so all their decisions weren't made by a stranger.

I read somewhere that women who have less pubic hair have a higher sex drive. Any truth to the story?

The distribution, quantity, and texture of pubic hair have a lot to do with your genetic and ethnic background. Some groups have very little body and pubic hair, some have a lot, and some have almost none at all. None of this has any correlation whatsoever to who is having the most sex, or who wants to have the most sex.

There are a number of theories about the purpose of pubic hair. One idea is that it's made to be a springy cushion between you and your partner, to lessen the friction and absorb the shocks as your two bodies are bouncing together. Since most of the parts of your body with hair also have a distinct odor, another theory is that it is the result of an evolutionary process to do with concentrating pheromones for attracting mates to propagate the species. A third school of thought (and the one to which I personally subscribe) has it that pubic hair is purely decorative. And a fourth, somewhat less serious idea is that just as eyebrows are built to keep the dust and grime from your eyes, so pubic hair is made to catch crumbs before they end up in your privates.

If, in the face of the scientific research, you are a woman who still believes your hair-down-there will affect your sex drive, there's a simple experiment you can perform: shave it off, and see what happens. Just be sure you're careful what you cut, and be sure to use a good skin moisturizer afterward to prevent the discomfort of razor burn.

Q I have friends who talk about ten, fifteen, or twenty orgasms in a row. I only have one. Is there something wrong with me?

A There was a time when it was believed only a small proportion of women were multi-orgasmic. The data have been updated several times since then, but many women still find that one orgasm is just right, thank you very much, even if they are indeed capable of having more.

There is nothing in particular that stops a woman from having more than one orgasm at a time, unlike men, whose bodies require some rest between events. What happens is that after the first, a woman can slide down to a plateau stage, then rise up to another orgasm. Some use vibrators or other sex toys to create a series. This can sometimes backfire, though, as some women then find it difficult to achieve orgasms with a source that doesn't shake, rattle, and roll at 15,000 r.p.m.

Q When my boyfriend and I make love, I occasionally hear sounds erupting from my vagina. It embarrasses me no end. Why does this happen, and what can I do to prevent it?

A Not all women have an audible vagina, but it's hardly a rare phenomenon, especially if you make love in a position in which your pelvis is elevated. This is because the acoustic event has to do with the position of your uterus and vagina creating a vacuum during sex. When air is expelled back out the opening, you hear the familiar sound. You might try changing positions to make this go away.

Another possibility is simply that the piston-like motion of sex is forcing air in and out, again creating those flapping noises. Either way, the sounds are completely normal, and you have nothing to worry about. If changing positions doesn't help, I'd suggest you develop a sense of humor about your auditory accompaniments. If it still bothers you, just crank up the stereo.

Is it true you should not go swimming while having your period?

You can go swimming any time you like. This sexual myth goes back to the bad old days when physicians treated a woman's period as if it were an illness. The water in a swimming pool will not get inside your private parts and wreak havoc, just because you're having your period. If this were true, you wouldn't be able to have a bath at that time of the month, either.

See-through and super-tight clothes are all the rage for women these days. My question is, here in our politically correct atmosphere, is it okay to look, or do I risk being charged with sexual harassment?

I say look all you want. I get really annoyed when women wear clothes that expose their body parts, then get indignant when men look at them. As far as I'm concerned, if you don't want things to be inspected, don't hold them out on public display — that's like framing an awesome painting, then telling people they can only gaze at the wall on which it is hung. Just consider the huge sales of pushup wonderbras. They're designed to create maxi-cleavage with mini-breasts. Why would any woman want that unless she wanted to be looked at? Just remember, guys — looking doesn't mean leering, and it most certainly doesn't mean touching.

What exactly is a yeast infection, and how do you get one?

Yeast is a regular resident of the vaginal tract, one of many micro-organisms that make their normal homes in the human body. It only becomes a problem when the numbers multiply and produce a discharge, which can have a noticeable odor and cause unbearable itching. Basically, the infection is the result of a yeast population explosion. This yeast baby boom can be caused by the pH balance of the vagina being thrown off-kilter by anything from antibiotics to stress. It can seem to happen for no particular reason at all.

A yeast infection is not considered a sexually transmitted disease, though in certain stubborn cases, the doctor may treat both partners. The good thing is, there's a quick remedy you can get from your doctor or pharmacist. It usually takes a couple of days to work, and that will be that. The bad thing is, you can always get another yeast infection. Sorry.

I'm twenty-three years old, and I consider myself a pretty normal woman. Would you consider me abnormal if I like to have sex all the time and I think about it a lot?

A Perhaps if you were ninety-three, it would be unusual. Since you fall between the ages of eighteen and forty-five, probably not. According to one survey, men on average think about sex once every six minutes, every waking hour of every day. Women probably aren't far behind, if at all.

If you're in a sexual relationship with someone who really turns you on, perhaps you just see sex everywhere — in the trees across the street and the oranges on your breakfast table. If that sounds right, I say party on.

On the other hand, if you're having sex or thinking about sex continuously, to the exclusion of all else, then you may be confusing a desire for closeness and intimacy with a desire for sex.

The bottom line here is if you're having lots of sex and enjoying it, that's great. If the frequency of your sexual activity is interfering with your relationships to the point where you're worrying about it, then maybe something else is going on. In that case, you might consider the state of your self-esteem, your need for intimacy, or a fear of losing the person with whom you're involved. Ask yourself how you feel about your sex drive. Merely having a strong one is not a disease.

12

Foul Play

Lots of problems revolving around sex appear monumental to the person concerned, but once set in perspective, or placed into the past, they often seem less than overwhelming, and we wonder why we were so upset in the first place. On the other hand, there are other areas involving sex in which the risks are all too real, and the solutions much more difficult to come by.

You seem pretty liberal about sex. My question is, are there any sexual practices that are bad ideas, no matter what?

A I can think of a few right off the top of my head. For starters, incest is a very bad idea at any time. Family is one of the places where people really care about you and have a lifelong relationship with you. If you add sexuality to the mixture, you often create a lifetime of emotional scars as well. Sexual relationships within the family are harmful, and should never be encouraged or attempted.

Autoerotic asphyxiation is another bad idea. There are people who think that pressing on the carotid artery and cutting off the oxygen to the brain at the time of orgasm will make it more powerful. (The use of amyl nitrate — so-called "poppers" — creates a similar result.) Interrupting the supply of oxygen to your brain at any time is dangerous. Risking death in a dubious quest for a better orgasm is always a bad idea.

I also think you should be wary of any practice involving bondage, since it can also lead to unwanted, unfortunate results, especially when you don't know your partner extremely well, or when one person is placed in a position of powerlessness.

Q **I work part-time as a waitress in my parents' restaurant, and I have this problem with a few older men. They try to put their hands on me when I'm taking orders, and take every opportunity to wink or make some gross comment about my clothes. This is a small town, and I can't risk my parents' livelihood by telling off the customers. Is there a way to get them to stop harassing me?**

A The first people you should approach are your parents — they should be your allies in this battle. Next time you make the rounds taking orders, take your father with you. He can say something along the lines of, "How are you guys today? Have you met my daughter? Isn't she sweet? She's the apple of my eye." This approach will leave your lecherous patrons wondering whether he's just a proud papa or a concerned father delivering a subtle message about what kind of behavior is acceptable in his restaurant.

There's this guy who watches me from his bedroom window every day and sometimes at night. I have no idea what he's doing as I can only see his head. I feel like I don't have enough reason to call the police, and I don't want to move. What can I do?

What's going on here? I presume the only reason he can see you is that your windows are uncovered. Meanwhile, you can only see his head? Who's watching whom? If you feel there's something threatening about this guy, check into the anti-stalking laws that are going into effect all over the continent. If he doesn't seem dangerous, the quick and easy solution is venetian blinds or curtains. Put them up and the show's over.

About prostitution — if a guy is unmarried and doesn't have a girlfriend and doesn't want to masturbate, then what other option is there? As long as using prostitutes doesn't become an obsessive habit, how can it be such a terrible thing under these circumstances?

Consider this: experts say that approximately 80 percent of the women working as prostitutes "choose" their profession as the result of being victims of child sexual abuse. This means eight out of ten of the women you're sleeping with were abused as children.

Still turn you on? Then think about this: there are precious few things a person owns outright in his or her life. Your emotions and your body are two of the few, so it's a sad situation when a person is willing to let go of one, merely because someone has the right amount of cash.

What I suggest is that you take a long look at your choice of sex partners. You are not going to learn how to have good sex from them, and you certainly aren't going to find a girlfriend. Finally, before you write off masturbation as an alternative, consider the advantages: you'll save money, there's no way you'll catch a disease, and you won't have to dress up for it.

My girlfriends and I got talking about rape, and whether it's more common now than when we were kids. What constitutes rape, and is it on the increase?

First of all, the very term "rape" is going the way of the dinosaur. It's still clinging to life in some jurisdictions, but for the most part it's been killed off by a new legal category: sexual assault (alias sexual battery). The change may seem semantic, but it isn't. It reflects the modern view that sexual assaults are more about power and control than sexuality. The classification shift is a healthy one, but unfortunately, sexual assault remains a vastly underreported category of crime. For that reason, the statistics are difficult to analyze. An increase in the apparent rate of sexual assault may mean only that more victims are willing to press charges these days, as compared with years gone by.

If you were molested at age five, and having flashbacks at age twenty, and you now remember that it was your father who did the molesting, can you still prosecute him?

A Statutes of limitation vary from one legal jurisdiction to another, so it would depend on where the molestation took place, and on what laws were in effect at the time. Regardless of whether you can have your father arrested, you should be talking with someone about your experiences. A counselor might be as much help to you now as a prosecutor.

Q **Starting when I was twelve, I had sex with an older man — a minister — for two years. I thought it was a mutual thing, but now I realize he was taking advantage of me. My husband wants me to press charges. Part of me wants to, but part of me wants to forget the whole thing. What do you think?**

A You may want to start by contacting an organization that deals with people who have had sex abuse in their past. Speak to a counselor there who can help you make the decision to proceed or not, and who can refer you to a legal professional who can explain your options under the law. The most important part of this process is to deal with the unresolved feelings from the abuse itself. It's great that your husband is supportive and wants you to press charges, but the decision has to be yours, and if you decide to put it behind you without action, he'll have to accept your decision. Since you were a child at the time, I strongly recommend that you file a report with the local police, even if you choose not to pursue charges yourself. Sadly enough, predatory pedophiles almost always have a series of victims, and even though your own abuse may be long in the past, this man's criminal behavior may still be occurring today.

Q I'm nineteen, and I'm dating a girl who's fourteen going on twenty-one, if you know what I mean. What are the legal consequences of having sex under the age of consent?

A As with other legal questions, the answer to this one depends on the law in the state, province, or country in which you live. In Canada, for example, there is no actual age of consent, but an adult is breaking the law if he or she has sex with a minor. In other words, while two thirteen-year-olds having sex may not be a smart or safe thing, it is not illegal. On the other hand, if a thirty-five-year-old has intercourse with a twelve-year-old, the adult faces a charge of sexual assault, because minors cannot legally give consent to sex.

In the United States, although the penalties of having sex with a minor may vary from one jurisdiction to another, federal law makes it a serious crime if you cross a state line while finding a location for your illicit tryst. Elsewhere in the world, the reaction to consensual sex involving minors can range from a smirk and a giggle to the death penalty.

Q I have my own successful business, and I'm happily married with two kids. Eight years ago, when I was single, I had an affair with my secretary. I heard from her recently, and she says she wants money or she'll charge me with sexual harassment and wrongful dismissal. I don't know whether to ignore her, get a lawyer, go to the police, tell my wife. Help!

A Your ex-secretary has a new vocation: extortionist. It is a profession that comes with an interesting reward: prison time. Yes, you should call the police. This is one time when the movies don't lie — when you pay a blackmailer, they just keep coming back for more until they bleed you dry. Yes, you're probably going to have to explain the situation to your wife, but as you were single at the time, this shouldn't be a major problem. You did nothing wrong, and therefore you should act accordingly. If possible, you should try to get your ex-secretary's voice on tape, explaining what she wants from you (a pocket, voice-activated mini-recorder should work). This will provide backup for your side of the story when you see the police, and put a quick end to allegations of harassment and wrongful dismissal. After that, you can decide whether you want to charge *her* with harassment — a little bonus for her new career.

At a convention in Las Vegas last year, I had an encounter with a hooker. It's the first (and last) time I've ever been unfaithful to my partner. I feel guilty and I want to come clean, but I'm afraid she'll go off the deep end. Any suggestions?

First you have to decide whether coming clean will make you feel better and your partner feel worse. In this case, you are merely shifting the discomfort from you to her. If it was a one-time occurrence and you took precautions to prevent STDs and pregnancy, then I'd probably suggest you keep your lapse to yourself. You might want to sit down and write a long letter to your partner, detailing your feelings of guilt and remorse, how you resolve to never do anything like that again, and how you decided *not* to tell her to spare her feelings. Then put the sealed letter in a safe place instead of giving it to her. Buy her an expensive present and give her that instead, just because she's so wonderful. If she ever finds out on her own, you'll have the letter ready, and you can pray she'll understand and forgive you. I realize this advice is not going to sit well with a lot of people, but it's far too easy to be indignant and demand honesty when you're a bystander. My position is that in an instance like this, if there's any suffering to be done, it should be done by you, not by your wife.

My boyfriend is pressuring me to get my tongue pierced and wear a stud, because he says it will make oral sex better. I want to please him, but the idea really scares me. What should I do?

First ask yourself for whom it's going to make oral sex better: him or you. Then perhaps you can let him know you like oral sex just fine the way it is — with your tongue intact. Anything that scares you is best avoided, and no one should be pressured by anyone into something they fear, or with which they are even just mildly uncomfortable. He's got parts — let him puncture his own.

Make no mistake, body piercing is surgery, plain and simple. Worse yet, it is surgery performed by amateurs. Anyone with a spare set of clamps and a couple of sharp objects can call themselves a body piercer, with or without qualifications or hygienic conditions. There are no regulatory bodies for this "profession." You can suffer nerve damage, infection, or worse, and in the case of tongue piercing, you could easily end up with a permanent inability to form some speech sounds. Is a bit of gold flashing from the inside of your mouth worth risking an irreparable speech impediment? If the answer is yes, go ahead. If you think not, but you still want a flashy smile, try asking your dentist to replace one of your white ceramic fillings with gold.

I'm twenty-five years old, and I've always liked dangerous sex. I like to have my man play with knives while he's playing with me. I like the feel of cold steel against my skin, and it has to be

sharp and risky, or I'm just not turned on. I really love my current boyfriend, but he's having a hard time with my urges. I truly can't seem to get turned on any other way, but I don't want to lose him. What can I do?

A Everybody has their own arousal system, and no two work exactly alike, but yours is unfortunately at one of the extremes of the spectrum. When you start to put yourself in danger of being skewered on a butcher knife, it's hardly going to be a great capper to a romantic evening — especially when your partner is not a weapons expert, and doesn't feel comfortable obliging you.

I'd like to be able to suggest that if cold steel is your turn-on, you try a serving spoon, but it seems the lack of sharp edges would make it an unsatisfactory replacement. I think you need to see a counselor, and try to find out how you began associating mortal danger with sex in the first place. I don't know if you can work out a change in your attraction to high risk, or even if you want to, but I do know the gamble you're taking may be higher than you think. You could easily find yourself with a different kind of partner some time in the future, one who will be happy to oblige you with the knives, but who may take this deadly game further than even you desire.

Q I'm in my late thirties, with three children, and I've been married for ten years to the same man. My problem is that my husband believes it is my duty to sleep with him whenever he wants, regardless of how I feel about it. If I don't jump into bed whenever he wants, he just pushes me there. Once after an argument, he tied me up. Despite all this, I still care for him, even though he scares me sometimes. What should I do?

A You can start by explaining that your wonderful wedding ceremony did not give him the entitlement to have sex with you whenever and wherever he wants, regardless of your own interest in the activity. If necessary, remind him that in most jurisdictions today, the consent of both parties is required, married or not, or the result is a crime. To put it in less legalistic terms, you are not an object. You are a person, and your wishes must be taken into account, not just his.

The fact that he is unrelenting to the point of tying you up points to his having deeper and darker places that need to be examined. What are his feelings about women in general, not just his wife? What are his opinions about the sharing of personal power in a relationship? My guess would be that either he was brought up believing he could always get his own way, or he has a history of indeed getting his own way on the vast majority of occasions. Your three small children complicate your situation, as does the fact that you still care about him. With those conditions in mind, I'd say you have to make it clear to him that he has no right to be forcing himself upon you, and if necessary, that you will follow this up with legal advice. Take whatever steps are necessary to put an end to it. If you can, get him into some kind of counseling to deal with his problem — that would certainly be helpful to your entire family. Be certain of one thing: this is not a problem you can let slide or wish away. It is the kind of situation that often, if left alone, escalates into violence that can end in tragedy.

Q **I was molested when I was young, and I've now been happily married for over ten years. The problem is that the only way I can have an orgasm is by fantasizing about the stepfather who molested me. I had many years of counseling, which really helped, but this is the one thing I've never been able to overcome. I'm embarrassed and disgusted with myself. I love my husband and would prefer to be thinking about him. What can I do?**

A I think your problem lies more with your self-disgust over a fantasy than with the fantasy itself. It sounds like in most ways you've done really well with the unfair experiences you were dealt when you were younger. You're happily married, and seem to be having a great sex life with this one exception. I see two options for you here. The first is that you can re-frame what has happened to you — get a new perspective on the situation with which you can be more comfortable. Look at the fact that you cannot change history, and as far as sex goes, you were handed a lemon that you have now turned into lemonade. In other words, you've taken a bad experience and used it to get something pleasurable for yourself.

Your second option is to seek further counseling about your inability to live with this one last reminder of the past. Although you've already gone for counseling to deal with the abuse itself, sometimes you need to get to a different level to put the last parts of a problem behind you.

In any case, remember that your fantasies are personal, and no one but yourself needs to know what they are. Although your images may be disturbing you, remember you aren't exactly alone — most people's wildest fantasies also include scenarios they would never want to see on the six-o'clock news.

Q About two years ago, I left a relationship where my boyfriend was always manipulative, often angry, and mostly concerned with his own needs at the expense of mine. I think I understand why I stayed with him as long as I did, and I've moved on in my life, but I can't seem to forget the bad times with my ex-boyfriend, and I find myself dwelling on things I should have said or done. Why can't I let go of the past?

A I think it's impossible to leave any relationship completely behind you. You can leave the furniture and divide up the CD collection, but you have to take some memories. Some people treat them like baggage that has to be dragged behind. I prefer to think of them as tossed into a small backpack with comfortable shoulder straps, leaving your hands free to get on with life. If your pack contains memories you don't want to carry forever, your options are to find someone to get it off your back, or to find a path big enough for you to travel, but too small for those nasty memories.

Why don't you try writing down some of your thoughts, especially the zingy retorts you wish you'd used, and then bury the notebook, literally. You can rest assured that if you ever need them again, they'll be there waiting. Then you can give yourself permission to forget. Just remember you are the sum of all your experiences — including the lousy ones. No doubt there were some nice moments in this old relationship, so keep some spaces reserved for those. Then get on with your life. In another ten years, I guarantee he'll occupy a much smaller piece of your memory bank.

Q **I have a friend who was sexually abused as a child, and she says I have all the same problems that she does, and was probably abused as well. This is the second time someone has said this to me, so I'm starting to wonder, even though I have absolutely no memory of any kind of abuse. There were times in my childhood that weren't exactly picture perfect, but could I really somehow be blocking parts of my past from my memory?**

A It is indeed possible to block old memories — it's something everyone does in one way or another. The time you were mean to your best friend at age ten is probably something you've managed to forget, along with that time you stole something from the corner grocery store. Forgetting is also an integral part of forgiving, so sometimes we intentionally let go of the past.

As for dredging up memories that are no longer in plain sight, I can think of only two reasons why you'd want to: either to entertain yourself by rerunning great moments in your mind, or to learn something from past experiences, good or bad. Why flog yourself with the unpleasant past that you've already managed to put behind you? Just because your friend (who I assume is not a practicing counselor) has given you her amateur diagnosis of repressed abuse does not make it so. In her case, it may be that misery really does want company, or she may mean well but still be off base.

If you feel you have something to gain from counseling, by all means go. Your counselor may address your problems from a vastly different angle, and one that has nothing to do with digging up old memories that may not even exist.

Q I'm a university art student, and one of my classes uses nude models as subjects. Most of these models are male and female students making some extra money and seem perfectly comfortable being naked in front of the class. However, the professor who teaches the class seems to have a peculiar "thing" about one woman model, and is always trying to get her into poses that seem more exhibitionist than artistic, if you know what I mean. The situation makes a few of us more than a little uncomfortable, even though the model doesn't seem to complain. Should we do something, or butt out?

A I think it's perfectly reasonable to approach your instructor and ask why he finds it necessary to pose certain models in certain ways. If you can have the conversation in private in his office, you can let him know that from where you sit, his interest in one particular model seems different from his interest in the rest. You are entitled to let him know that the situation makes you uncomfortable, regardless of how the model herself feels, and your professor is entitled to give you his reasons. See what he says. I doubt very much that he's going to try to flunk you for asking, especially since your artistic talents will speak for themselves.

As a child, I was molested by a neighbor up the block. I'm nineteen now, and have never had a true, loving relationship with a man. My current boyfriend has asked me if I'm a virgin. Am I?

According to the technical definition of the word, you are not a virgin. However, if you choose, you can still tell your boyfriend you are sexually inexperienced. If your only experience happened without your consent, you can also tell him you've never made love — it will be the truth.

I have a twenty-year-old girlfriend, and I've been getting calls from a thirteen-year-old friend of a friend. She says she loves me and wants to sleep with me. These calls have been going on for three years, and now my problem is I'm starting to have feelings for her. The thing is she's only thirteen and I'm twenty-six. What should I do?

If these calls have been going on for three years, they started when she was ten, and you would have been better off doing something back then. By taking her calls for three years, you have been encouraging her, and since you are the adult in this situation, it's up to you to make the adult decisions. By letting this go on so long, you have complicated matters for yourself, since now she is a teenager (just barely), and perhaps starting to look less like a child. Remember that no matter how her body may be changing, she is still a child, not a woman. Sex with a child is offensive, and a criminal offense in most places. You should not be flattered by her attention: there must be something going on in her family for her to be reaching out to you in a way that is so inappropriate for her age. If you are indeed a friend, it's up to you to get a handle on this situation, either by talking to her parents about it, or to the friend you have in common — assuming the friend is not also thirteen years old.

I have been horribly bruised and abused by the sexual advances of my man, to the point of being totally turned off the minute he touches me. I tell him to stop hurting me, but he just says, "You like it." To me this is animal-like sex and not love. Despite all this, I still love him — I just want him to stop pushing me around. What do you think?

I think you should be very suspicious of a person who says he know your feelings better than you do, despite the fact that you're yelling differently. You say you're still in love with this man, but you sound more like an indentured slave than a partner. I think you have gotten used to the way he treats you — which is poorly — and you're misreading this as affection. What you describe is a controlling behavior that feeds his needs, but not your own. You have to take a long, hard look at a person who treats you so badly and won't listen when you repeatedly ask him to do things differently.

You may be too confused or disorganized to get yourself out of this situation, in which case you'd be better off getting to a safe place away from this abusive person's control. There are many women's shelters and counseling centers where you can get help. Don't put it off because you think you don't know where to go.

Once you feel more secure about your own safety, then you can figure out if you really do still love this man. If you decide there is a relationship here to build on, you can suggest to him that you go for counseling together, to try to repair what's already been torn apart. It's important you work through this process *before* you get back together, if in fact that's what you decide to do. It's never a good idea to remain in a situation where your physical safety is constantly at risk.

Life is what happens to you when you're waiting around for other things. Perhaps the question we should all ask ourselves from time to time is, "What if I only had six months to live? Would I be with this man? Would I be doing these activities, this job? Are these the friends with whom I would choose to spend my time?" If the answer to one or more is no, then take a long look around your life, and try to judge which things you'd really like to fix. Then, get after them, because this is your life, not a dress rehearsal. As far as we know, it's the only one we get. Use it wisely and lovingly, and place yourself in the company of those who really care about you, and laugh at your jokes, just like me.

Acknowledgments

With thanks to the people who helped to make this book happen:

Dr. David Freeman
Dr. Norm Hirt
Avery Raskin
Gary Ross
Erroll Jang
David Yager
Matthew White

Index